# BRONX BUMMERS

The Unofficial History
of the New York Yankees'
Bad Boys, Blunders and Brawls

## Robert Dominguez
### and David Hinckley

For more information contact:
Riverdale Avenue Books
5676 Riverdale Avenue
Riverdale, NY 10471.

www.riverdaleavebooks.com

Design by www.formatting4U.com
Cover by Scott Carpenter

Cover photos courtesy of the *New York Daily News*:
Babe Ruth takes Yankees manager Miller Huggins for a spin in 1921.
Thurman Munson collides with Red Sox catcher Carlton Fisk, 1973.
Jack McDowell salutes the Stadium crowd, 1995.
Background: Yankee Stadium on opening day, 1970

Digital ISBN: 978-1-62601-274-5
Print ISBN: 978-1-62601-275-2

First Edition April 2016

# Table of Contents

## Part I - Bad Boys

## Part II - Brawls

## Part III - Blunders

# Part I
**Bad Boys**

# Chapter One
## Where It All Began: "Big Bill" Devery and the Team that Graft Built

Even with two suspensions, one conviction and a well-deserved reputation as baseball's biggest blowhard, George Steinbrenner at his worst was practically a saint compared to the sinner that was William Stephen Devery, the original co-owner of the New York Yankees and one of the game's biggest rascals in an era when you couldn't swing a dead bat without hitting one.

New York's last chief of police was a man of distinction by title only—considering his position and the ill-gotten gains he's said to have amassed over his more than 20-year career as a civil servant, Devery was widely considered the most crooked cop the city has ever seen.

"Big Bill," as he was known in the mostly impolite society he ran with, may have built enough of a fortune to bankroll a baseball team in a major market like New York, but he was hardly your typical turn-of-the-century captain of industry.

Devery, all six feet and near 300 pounds of him, was a self-made man; a tough, street smart, cigar-chomping, Manhattan-born son of Irish-Catholic immigrants who tended bar in Bowery dives until he moved up in the sordid world that was hardscrabble Manhattan of the late 19th century.

Corpulent, charismatic and inherently corrupt, he lifted himself up from his humble beginnings the way many first-generation Irishmen of his time did: by lining the pockets of a crooked Tammany Hall politician. For the princely sum of $300, Devery bought his way into the New York Police Department as a patrolman.

Big Bill's rise up the NYPD ranks wasn't only swift, it was lined with dollars and sprinkled with gold dust. In a city powered by Tammany Hall's vast political machine, an industrious fellow like Devery, who had no qualms about openly milking a system that ran on graft, corruption and greed, was in his glory.

To say Devery—who joined the force in 1878 and made captain about a dozen years later—would make a nice return on his $300 is an understatement. His stubby fingers were in just about every dirty deal, kickback and bribe that went on in his domain. He lorded over the 22nd precinct on Manhattan's West Side, which encompassed a huge swath of the infamous "Tenderloin District" rife with brothels, gambling dens, dance halls and illegal after-hour joints whose proprietors were more than willing to grease the proper palms to stay open.

Devery, who took command of the precinct in 1893, immediately showed his men who was boss.

"They tell me there's a lot of graftin' going on in this precinct," he supposedly told the assembled horde at his inaugural address.

"Now that's going to stop! If there's any graftin' to be done, I'll do it."

Devery did, and then some. Word was that if you needed the big guy to look the other way for something or other, you'd pay a visit to his tailor, who would make you a custom-made suit for a cool $1,000—about $28,000 today. Big Bill, puffing on his ever-present stogie, would amble along later to collect before kicking up part of the grand to his Tammany patrons.

Needless to say, there were plenty of well-dressed crooks strolling the streets of Manhattan in those days.

Unfortunately for Devery, one can't be so blatant about "any graftin' to be done" without attracting the unwanted attention of actual law-abiding officials. He was indicted and tried several times for charges that included bribery and extortion—and skated each time.

Despite a sketchy reputation forged by newspaper coverage that simultaneously reviled and revered the always-quotable Devery, he was amply rewarded for his alleged sins. In 1898, a Tammany puppet-mayor appointed him chief of police; the proverbial fat rat was now in charge of the cheese factory.

It took another three years before Devery would be knocked off his lofty perch by an incoming, reform-minded mayor bent on ending corruption—the chief of police title would be forever abolished—but Big Bill would soon be on his way to much bigger things.

In 1903, he and a partner, an old pal and "businessman" named Frank J. Farrell, paid $18,000 for the Baltimore Orioles of the nascent American League of Professional Baseball Clubs—aka the American League—and shipped the franchise north, where it was renamed the New York Highlanders.

Farrell was a businessman, all right, just not a particularly upstanding one. Like Devery, he was born into an Irish-Catholic immigrant family in Manhattan, worked as a bartender in West Side saloons where Tammany Hall officials were regulars, and made plenty of friends among the political powers-that-be.

Unlike Devery, whom he had befriended over their common backgrounds and Tammany ties, Farrell would make his fortune as a saloon owner before eventually becoming one of the city's most notorious gambling hall operators and bookmakers—"The Pool Room King," as the papers dubbed him.

Granting ownership to a pair of disreputable characters was a sign of how desperate American League officials were to establish a successful franchise in New York to compete against the Giants and the more established National League.

Which would explain why Devery, despite his larger-than-life persona, was pretty much a silent partner during the 13 years he co-owned the team with Ferrell. In fact, his lengthy *New York Times* obituary of June 21, 1919, when Devery at 63 died of "apoplexy" at his lavish mansion in Rockaway, Queens, doesn't once mention his Highlander/Yankee ties.

Ferrell wisely laid low as well and left the daily running of the Highlanders to club president Joseph Gordon, at least publicly. Both Ferrell and Devery were no-shows at the Highlanders' first press conference before the 1903 season.

That changed the next year, when Ferrell— foreshadowing Steinbrenner's tumultuous reign decades later—would become a hands-on owner known for hiring, firing and feuding with his managers and players.

Not surprisingly, the Devery/Farrell years weren't particularly successful. After nearly capturing the AL pennant in 1904 in just their second season, the Highlanders were mostly a second-division club that struggled to attract crowds. The hearts and wallets of New York baseball fans, at least until a pitcher-turned outfielder named Babe Ruth came to town, belonged to the powerhouse Giants.

By the start of the 1915 season, the cash-strapped partners had sold the team to another pair of moneyed men who presumably acquired their fortunes legally: beer baron Col. Jacob Ruppert, an ex-congressman and National Guard officer, and a former U.S. army engineer with the colorful moniker of Capt. Tillinghast L'Hommideau Huston.

Devery and Farrell didn't have a pennant, let alone a World Series championship to show for their 13 years of ownership—Ruth, and the first of 40 American League flags, were still more than five years away.

But the original partners, under whose stewardship the team officially came to be known as the Yankees, made a killing off their $18,000 investment. They split the $460,000 sale to Ruppert and Huston, though the old friends hadn't been on speaking terms for years.

Both men would soon fade into obscurity—and both went to their graves relatively broke. Farrell, who died of a heart attack in 1926 in an Atlantic City hotel, was worth a little over $1,000 when he went—or just enough for a custom suit at Devery's tailor.

Devery was $1,000 in the red when he died in the

*Robert Dominguez & David Hinckley*

summer of 1919 and wouldn't live to see the infamous "Black Sox" World Series, a bribery scandal the infamous police chief would have surely appreciated.

6

## Chapter Two
### The Tabasco Kid

As far as baseball nicknames go, no player ever lived up to his moniker like one Norman Arthur Elberfeld, aka "The Tabasco Kid."

A member of the first-ever Yankees team in 1903—back when they were known as the Highlanders—Elberfeld was undoubtedly the toughest, orneriest ballplayer of his or any era. A shortstop who stood just 5' 7" and weighed barely 160 pounds, he forged a reputation as a fearless, aggressive competitor who was famously described as the "dirtiest, scrappiest, most pestiferous, most rantankerous, most rambunctious ball player that ever stood on spikes."

No, going by Norman just wouldn't do for a player of his ill-tempered ilk, which is why another Deadball Era scribe slapped Elberfeld with the "Tabasco" sobriquet in honor of his "peppery" style of play.

Just how dirty, scrappy and pestiferous was the Kid? It's said he once gave a rookie a lesson in the dangers of sliding into a base face-first the youngster never forgot. As the player plowed into second, Elberfeld buried his knee into the back of his neck and ground his face in the dirt.

The rookie, a Detroit Tiger outfielder named Ty

Cobb—who would eventually prove to be no shrinking violet himself—would never again slide headfirst into a base.

Putting a rookie in his place was just routine baseball business compared to some of Elberfeld's more legendary antics. The Kid, an Ohio native who broke in with the Philadelphia Phillies in 1898, had an his instant dislike for anyone wearing the uniform of the opposing team that was only surpassed by his hatred for the men in blue.

As a minor leaguer, he once ended an argument with an umpire by tossing dirt into the ump's open mouth. As a member of the Tigers in 1900, a year before the team joined the nascent American League, the hot-tempered shortstop was given the thumb three times in a span of eight games.

Elberfeld wasn't all mouth, though. By all accounts, he had a cannon for an arm and an inherent fearlessness when it came to turning the double play. He missed most of the 1908 season with the Highlanders after getting spiked, and would spend the last years of his career wearing shin guards made of whalebone to protect legs shredded by opponents tearing into second with spikes high and sharpened.

He also wasn't afraid to take one for the team— getting hit by a pitch was a big part of Elberfeld's arsenal. When he retired in 1914, he was sixth on the all-time list with 165 HBP (another Yankee shortstop, Derek Jeter, has since passed him).

Elberfeld may have been small and scrappy, but he would also develop into one of the best-hitting shortstops in any league, with only the immortal Honus Wagner considered a bigger threat at the plate at that position.

Yet as colorful as the Kid was, he had plenty of dog in him. When things didn't go his way—like, say, when he didn't like his manager, which happened often—Elberfeld's behavior could make Manny Ramirez look like the ultimate team player. Suspected of loafing by his manager in Detroit in order to force a trade, Elberfeld was fined, suspended and eventually sent packing to the brand-new New York Highlanders in the middle of the 1903 season.

While the fledgling A.L. team played in the shadow of the powerful Giants, Elberfeld flourished in the New York spotlight, his exploits chronicled by the huge and highly competitive newspaper industry—it was there that a writer dubbed him the Tabasco Kid, a nickname reminiscent of a Mexican bandido. An arrest for throwing a bottle—or a knife, depending on which paper you read—at a hotel waiter only added to Elberfeld's rough-and-tumble reputation.

His occasional on-field tirades weren't limited to the men in blue. The Kid fought openly with several teammates, Highlanders outfielder Wid Conroy being a particular nemesis and frequent target of Elberfeld's quick fists.

That feistiness, though, would end up helping to cost the young Highlander team a shot at their first pennant in 1906. With the team in a tight race for first place with the Chicago White Sox, Elberfeld—who, by the way, was named team captain that year, the second in Yankees history—got into a memorable scrap with home plate umpire Silk O'Loughlin the papers could only describe as "disgraceful."

Elberfeld, upset over O'Loughlin's having called a runner safe in an early September game against the

Philadelphia Athletics, took his disagreement with the call a bit too far—he repeatedly tried to spike the umpire with his baseball shoes. It took a trio of city cops to get Elberfeld off the field, who then refused to leave the Highlanders' Hilltop Park until he was made to realize his team would lose by forfeit.

The Kid's childish behavior resulted in a relatively light eight-game suspension, but it was enough to stall the Highlanders' pennant push. After having swept a record five doubleheaders in five games to that point, they just weren't the same team without their top-of-the-order sparkplug at short.

They finished the season three games behind the White Sox, and wouldn't even come close to sniffing first place for the next 15 seasons, when the arrival of Babe Ruth turned the franchise around.

Amazingly, it was Elberfeld's second run-in with O'Loughlin in less than a month. In an August 8 game, an irate Elberfeld had threatened the ump with his bat after O'Loughlin refused to reward him first base after the Kid insisted he had been hit by a pitch.

The fan favorite would become a pariah by the following season, when Elberfeld would once again be accused of laying down on his team. After a late July game in which he threw the ball away three times, a disgusted Highlander owner Frank Ferrell suspended his rogue shortstop.

Farrell, much like future Yankees owner George Steinbrenner was wont to do, took his complaints to the press. "For more than two weeks past, [Elberfeld] has refused to talk with other members of the team," said Farrell.

"He has declined to be rubbed by the trainer. He

has refused to play his best, as the public well knows. In short, he has acted in such a queer manner that if he had not been tampered with, he has gone daffy."

Not exactly the same as Boss George berating a lazy pitcher for being a "fat, pussy toad," but Farrell got his point across—and succeeded in getting the fans to turn against the former fan favorite. When the announcement of Elberfeld's suspension was made between games of a doubleheader, the crowd of 8,000 at Hilltop Park cheered heartily at the news.

Farrell, though, apparently had a soft spot for the fiery Elberfeld—sort of how Steinbrenner felt for another troubled, feisty Yankee infielder named Billy Martin, who would end up managing the team five times despite his sordid history.

A year after insinuating Elberfeld was either throwing games or just plain nuts, Farrell named the Kid to be player-manager about a third of the way into the 1908 season.

The Tabasco Kid responded with a horrendous 27-71 record at the helm, the first of only four last-place finishes in Highlander/Yankee history.

## Chapter Three
### The Prince of Darkness

The Yankees' first-ever, bonafide superstar was a good-looking, smooth-fielding singles hitter who combined Derek Jeter's charisma, Don Mattingly's glove work and Reggie Jackson's ego.

Hal Chase, the gifted first baseman who spent nearly nine years with the then-New York Highlanders during modern baseball's infancy, unfortunately had plenty of Pete Rose in him, too.

Chase was a lifetime .291 batter over 15 seasons, a solid clutch hitter and a good base stealer. But as soon as he joined the team in 1905, the 22-year-old rookie who would soon come to be known as "Prince Hal" set the standard for how defense-minded first sackers would play the position for generations to come.

He was, in baseball parlance, like a cat out there, known for his ability to pounce on bunts up the line, save his infielders countless throwing errors and snag just about any hard grounder that came his way.

For fans back then who cared to argue over who was the best first baseman in the game, it was a sure bet Chase would be their first choice—none other than

The Babe himself proclaimed there was no one better at the position.

Knowing what we do now, though, Prince Hal would have likely wagered against himself and walked away with a bundle.

Despite his range, reflexes and flair for highlight-reel plays—had there been highlight reels then—Chase sure made a lot of errors for such a defensive wizard. As a Highlander/Yankee, he averaged a horrific 30 miscues a season—his high was 36 in 1911—and his career total of 285 errors at first base is still the American League record.

By comparison, Mattingly, a nine-time Gold Glover, committed 64 career errors at the position over his 13 full seasons, an average of five per year.

Whether it was easy ground balls that should have been handled, or the throws from short that somehow popped out of his glove as the runner crossed the bag, Chase's erratic side always seemed to come at the wrong time.

Like, say, in the late innings, with the game on the line.

Which naturally prompted some observers to wonder whether New York's marquee player was tanking games.

That would come to include Chase's fed-up teammates and managers, several of who openly accused him of laying down. It didn't help team chemistry any that Chase was apparently a favorite of Highlander co-owner Frank Farrell, New York City's most notorious gambling hall owner and no angel himself. Chase, in fact, was named team captain from 1909-1912 despite his tainted reputation.

Farrell, who usually looked the other way when Chase made one of his late-inning blunders or went AWOL from the team—not an infrequent occurrence— actually fired manager George Stallings late in the 1910 season for having the audacity to question Chase's purported ties to gamblers.

In a surreal move that would have shocked even George Steinbrenner in his mercurial prime, Farrell promptly replaced Stallings with Chase, who became player-manager with about two weeks left in the season.

The Highlanders, a second-place team in '10 under Stallings, finished 1911 as a sixth-place, .500 club with Chase at the helm, 25.5 games out of first place.

Chase would eventually be run out of town. In 1913, new manager Frank Chance—the former Cubs first baseman immortalized in the poem, "Tinkers to Evers to Chance," about Chicago's famed double-play trio—pulled an unassisted force play on Chase and persuaded Farrell to trade his star for the good of the team.

Prince Hal managed to play another five seasons in the National League even as evidence mounted that he was either throwing games or trying to bribe teammates to do the same. But once the Black Sox Scandal of 1919 exposed the World Series was fixed, Chase was among the players caught up in new Commissioner Kenesaw Mountain Landis' purge of anyone with even the slightest stench of associating with gamblers.

Chase would spend his final years as a destitute, heavy drinker, a Depression-era drifter taking whatever odd job he could find. But the faded star made headlines again when he gave an interview to *The Sporting News* from a hospital bed weeks before his death in 1947, at age 64.

The so-called "Baseball Paper of the World" touted the exclusive with ads reading, "What has become of Hal Chase? Games greatest first sacker rues mistakes in relating history," and the story did indeed live up the hype.

In a shocking confession, Chase gave a detailed account of how rampant gambling was in baseball during his playing days, how in deep he was with gamblers—he wagered up to $100 a game, though, like Pete Rose decades later, he claimed he never bet against his own team—and how he was glad the game had been cleaned up.

But mostly, the former slick-fielding superstar spoke about how much he regretted the errors of his ways.

"I was foolish and all the stuff I thought was so smart only robbed me of the kind of life I should be living today," lamented Chase. "I was wrong, at least in most things, and my best proof is that I am flat on my back, without a dime.

"I'm the loser, just like all gamblers are. I lived to make great plays, but what did I gain? Nothing!"

# Chapter Four
## Ray Caldwell

He was a crafty, hard-throwing hurler who could hit almost as well as he could pitch, and just about everyone who saw Ray Caldwell play agreed he could've been one of the best there ever was had it not been for a few bad habits.

These included, but were likely not limited to, a hankering for liquor, loose women, late nights and larceny.

Not to mention a tendency to disappear from the team to indulge those habits.

A few years before a young Boston player named Babe Ruth started making a name for himself as an excellent pitcher, dangerous hitter and all-star carouser, Caldwell had already established himself as the New York Yankees' resident wild child whose flashes of Hall of Fame-caliber brilliance were interspersed with incidents of bad behavior.

Caldwell, nicknamed "Slim" for his tall and lanky build, broke in with the then-Highlanders late in 1910, then became a star the following season when he won 14 games and hit a respectable .272 while also seeing time as an outfielder.

But in a pattern that would be repeated countless times over his 12-year Major League career, Caldwell suffered through a string of arm injuries the next two seasons that limited his contributions to the team but left him with plenty of time to get into trouble. In one instance, failing to show up for a series in Boston earned Slim a fat fine of $250—about 10% of his salary—and an indefinite suspension.

By 1914, with the Highlanders now known as the Yankees, a healthy Caldwell became the team's ace. He chalked up 18 wins against 9 losses with a sparkling 1.94 ERA, 5 shutouts and 22 complete games.

Unfortunately, nearly all those wins came before August. On July 31, Caldwell was 17-7—singlehandedly accounting for 40% of the 42 games won by the Yankees, who were languishing in seventh place and 18 games back.

Yet he would soon pull another disappearing act, going AWOL on a road trip. Facing another formidable fine from fed-up manager Frank Chance, Caldwell decided to jump ship altogether in the middle of September—by joining a rival baseball league despite being under contract to the Yankees.

Caldwell was a huge headache and a public relations nightmare, to be sure—the papers weren't shy about clueing readers in to Caldwell's "occasional flirtation with that which is amber and foamy."

But winning pitchers who could also play the outfield and be counted on to get a key pinch hit were rare, and the Yankees were reluctant to let their recalcitrant ace get away. With $900 in fines hanging over his perpetually hung-over head, Caldwell convinced owner Frank Farrell to cancel the fines, and the pitcher was back in the fold (an action that likely led to Chance's abrupt resignation).

It was very nearly a storybook ending. After getting a hefty raise entering the 1915 season, Caldwell flourished under new manager "Wild Bill" Donovan. He earned his money and more by winning 19 games for a fifth-place team that only had 69 victories, while also smacking 4 home runs—the American League leader had 7—and knocking in 20 runs in only 144 at-bats.

Of course, this being Caldwell meant the good times couldn't last. An injury-plagued 1916 season resulted in a 5-12 record, two suspensions and a late-September stint in alcohol rehab followed by yet another bizarre disappearance over the winter.

After not being heard from for months, reporters got wind that Caldwell had been playing baseball in Panama under an assumed name. The pitcher, who showed up late for spring training in Florida, denied it and told anyone who'd listen that he had spent the winter in New York.

He couldn't, however, explain his tan.

By this point, his relationship with the Yankees was like a bad marriage in which one spouse keeps giving the other a string of last chances. Caldwell's 1917 season unfolded to a familiar script: a smattering of great performances, a handful of missed curfews, the inevitable fines and suspensions.

Except this time Caldwell added a touch of thievery to the mix. A St. Louis woman accused him of swiping her $150 diamond ring. The pitcher was hauled in for larceny but charges were dropped after the ring was returned.

The last straw for the Yankees finally came in 1918, after Caldwell called in sick for a mid-August game. In a ploy to avoid being drafted during World War I, Caldwell jumped ship again and took a job with a New Jersey shipbuilding company—workers in certain industries that supplied the U.S. military were exempt from being called up. Caldwell's job, though, consisted of playing for the company baseball team.

That winter he was the biggest name in a seven-player deal that packed him and his troubles to Boston, where to no one's surprise he quickly wore out his welcome and was released by August. It probably didn't help that one of his roommates was a 24-year-old pitcher named Babe Ruth, hardly a paragon of virtue and sobriety.

Caldwell, who by this time was one of the few Major Leaguers allowed to continue throwing a spitball, was picked up by the Cleveland Indians and would reward their faith with 20 wins in 1920, a season culminating in the Tribe's first World Series championship.

He may have been an immature boozer who squandered his talents, but no one can deny Caldwell was a gamer. His infamous off-the-field antics aside, he's perhaps best known for a strange occurrence that came after he joined the Indians in 1919.

Holding a 2-1 lead against the Philadelphia Athletics in a late August game, Caldwell was one out from the win when a sudden summer storm passed over the park. Spectators watched in horror as a bolt of lightning crackled and hit the pitcher's mound, knocking Caldwell unconscious.

After coming to, he electrified the crowd with a

rare display of guts few, if any, modern ballplayer would even consider—Caldwell insisted on staying in the game and got the final out.

# Chapter Five
**The Badass Bambino**

George Herman Ruth may have been baseball's biggest and most beloved star, but he was hands-down the game's all-time badass, too.

The seeds of his renegade, rebellious nature were planted early on. The man-child everyone the world over would come to know as the larger-than-life Babe was an inveterate truant and delinquent whose parents shipped off at age seven to St. Mary's Industrial School for Boys in Baltimore, a borderline reform school where George—deemed "incorrigible and vicious" and "beyond the control" of his parents—was raised by the Catholic Xaverian Brothers who practically preached baseball as religion.

"Looking back on my boyhood, I honestly don't remember being aware of the difference between right and wrong," the Babe once said, and that recklessness, bad behavior and devil-may-care attitude extended far into adulthood as the Bambino relished using his celebrity status to feed his insatiable twin appetites for hooch and hoochie mamas.

But take away his compulsive carousing, and Ruth still ranks as baseball's No. 1 bad boy, a man who perennially vied for the league lead in HR, RBI and STDs. For all his accomplishments on the field as both a premier pitcher and hitter, Ruth was also known for tangling with teammates, opponents, umpires and even fans in the stands, all the while taking pleasure in defying Yankee management and all-mighty baseball Commissioner Kenesaw Mountain Landis with antics that would have gotten him run out of New York had he played in the modern era.

Ruth, no angel in his years with the Boston Red Sox, turned up the notch on his wayward ways almost immediately after his purchase by the Yankees from the cash-strapped Sox for the then-spectacular sum of $125,000. The Yanks weren't even out of spring training in 1920, his first season with the team, when he ran into the stands after a heckler who then stopped Ruth in his tracks by pulling a knife on him.

It wouldn't be the last time someone brandished a weapon at him. Reporters covering the Yankees once bore witness to an angry, jilted ex-lover of the Babe holding a knife as she pursued him through a train, while another time the jealous husband of one of Ruth's countless paramours, armed with a pistol, chased him out of a hotel.

The 1922 season proved a particularly trouble-filled one for the Bambino, who followed up his greatest year ever, and arguably the best by any player in history—Ruth led the Yankees to their first-ever pennant with a staggering, then-record 59 HR, 168 RBI and a .378 average to go with 177 runs, 44 doubles, 16 triples and a still-record 457 total bases—with the unofficial record for most single-season fines and suspensions.

Chosen to be the Yankees' captain prior to the start of the season, Ruth didn't play for the first 33 games after Landis suspended him and fellow outfielder Bob Meusel for six weeks for violating league rules by going on an off-season barnstorming tour.

Ruth wasn't back in the lineup a week when he went into the stands after yet another heckler. The incident not only cost him a one-game suspension and fine, but manager Miller Huggins stripped his biggest star, an immature 27 at the time, of his captaincy.

It was probably a wise decision. Ruth was suspended twice more that year for arguing with umpires, and even got into a dugout tussle with teammate Wally Pipp (yes, *that* Wally Pipp, the star first baseman who in 1925 sat out one game and lost his job forever to a young Lou Gehrig).

It was inevitable that Ruth, who was legendary for his sexual stamina—it's said he sampled the entire staff of a St. Louis brothel in one long night, decades before Viagra—would end up mired in a sex scandal.

And he didn't disappoint. Late in 1922, Ruth was sued for $50,000 by a teenage shop girl who claimed Ruth got her pregnant, welched on his promise to marry her—and committed statutory rape to boot. He later settled out of court.

The so-called Sultan of Swat was also the Titan of Traffic Tickets, logging countless violations—and not a few fender-benders likely the result of DUI—and even spending an afternoon in jail for speeding on a Manhattan street.

The Babe being the Babe, he was sprung early from his one-day sentence so he could make the

Yankee game that day—Ruth's contract stipulated he'd be fined $500 for every game he missed.

Allowed to change into his uniform in his cell, he made it to the park in the middle of the game, thanks to a police motorcycle escort that zipped through the city faster than the ungodly 26 M.P.H. cops had accused Ruth of going in the first place.

# Chapter Six
## Jake Powell's Racist Radio Quote

For a ballplayer to utter the n-word on the radio was bad enough even in 1938, a decade before Jackie Robinson broke baseball's color line and a time when Jim Crow laws were the norm.

But it was the way Yankee outfielder Jake Powell said it that made it so much worse.

Powell, a native of Silver Spring, Md., already had a less-than-stellar reputation as a degenerate gambler and all-around ne'er-do-well when the fed-up Washington Senators traded him to the Yankees in 1936 despite his solid bat.

Among his more dubious baseball achievements was getting caught trying to steal anything that wasn't nailed down in his hotel room during a road trip. But ashtrays and towels weren't good enough for Powell. His attempted booty: the curtains, bedspread and a circular fan.

While with the Senators, Powell—apparently not very fond of Jews, either—broke Hank Greenberg's wrist by intentionally colliding with the Detroit Tigers' first baseman during a game early in 1936, ending the young slugger's season after just 12 games.

There's an old saying in baseball that the best trades are the ones that benefit both teams. The midseason deal between Washington and New York would prove to be a wash when the Yankees shipped their own dedicated bigot, Ben Chapman, to the Senators for Powell.

A Nashville-born outfielder, Chapman was a lifetime .300 hitter who history remembers more for a small mind than any big hits. He was infamous for taunting Jewish fans with the Nazi salute—this at a time when Germany's Jews were being persecuted and stripped of all rights.

Chapman would outdo himself years later, though. As the Philadelphia Phillies' manager, he would make Jackie Robinson's uneasy entrance to the Major Leagues a living hell by baiting him mercilessly from the bench.

The n-word likely being one of the nicer things Chapman called Robinson.

So despite the baggage Powell brought with him up north, the Yankees figured they were getting the better of the deal, a quite literal lesser of two evils.

And for a while, the trade looked like a winner. Powell, a scrappy hitter with speed, batted .302 in his half-season with the Bombers, sparking a powerhouse lineup that included Murderer's Row stalwarts Lou Gehrig and Tony Lazzeri, catcher Bill Dickey and a 21-year-old rookie sensation named Joe DiMaggio.

Powell also hit .455 in the '36 World Series against the Giants, the first of four straight championships for the Bombers.

But the good times didn't last. By 1938, Powell was a just a spare part on the steamroller that was the late-'30s Yankees when he sat for a radio interview before a July game against the White Sox at Chicago's Comiskey Park.

The conversation innocently veered towards what Powell did during the off-season; Powell answered that he was a cop in Dayton, Ohio.

It was after the announcer asked how Powell stayed in shape over the winter that the outfielder would utter the ugly line he would carry with him for the rest of his short, troubled life.

"I beat n-----s over the head with my blackjack," said Powell.

The firestorm started as soon as the words left his mouth. Calls from angry listeners flooded the radio station, while black community leaders stormed into Comiskey the next day demanding Powell be kicked out of the game for good.

They wouldn't get the lifetime ban they were seeking, but baseball commissioner Kenesaw Mountain Landis was under pressure to do *something*. So Powell, who of course denied saying anything derogatory—no tape exists of the interview—was slapped with a ten-day suspension.

Yet Powell had his defenders. More than a few baseball writers basically crossed the incident off to just Jake being Jake. Even the commissioner's official statement announcing the suspension sounded wishy-washy, coming as it did from the man who crowed about cleaning up baseball by banishing the 1919 Black Sox players from the game forever despite their acquittal on charges they threw the World Series.

Landis chalked up Powell's remark to being "due more to carelessness than intent."

The Yankees would soon rid themselves of Powell, who would play his last year in 1945 with the Phillies—where Chapman was the manager. One can only imagine how enlightened those late-night conversations at the hotel bar must've been between the two.

Three years later, Powell, drinking heavily and on the skids, would be arrested in Washington, D.C., for passing bad checks. He was 40 years old when he pulled out a pistol at the police station and shot himself dead.

# Chapter Seven
**Fritz & Susanne & Mike & Marilyn**

There's a reason the Yankees have been fairly consistent winners for nearly a century. Besides their collection of homegrown legends that anchored championship teams, just about every great Yankee era can be defined by a lopsided trade that was instrumental in bringing baseball glory to New York.

To wit: Hall of Fame pitchers Waite Hoyt in the 1920s and Red Ruffing in the '30s, who blossomed in the Bronx after coming from Boston; Roger Maris in 1960 for an aging Hank Bauer and a handful of no-names; sparkplug Mickey Rivers and No. 2 starter Ed Figueroa for one-year wonder Bobby Bonds in the '70s; right field stalwart Paul O'Neill for underachieving Roberto Kelly in the '90s.

But no trade shook New York to its core—not to mention baseball and some of the more conservative parts of the nation, too—like the blockbuster that was announced during spring training in 1973 involving two popular Yankee pitchers.

On a warm day in Fort Lauderdale in early March, Fritz Peterson, the team's top lefty starter, and fellow southpaw Mike Kekich went public with a shocking little secret most of their teammates had been wise to for months.

Peterson and Kekich—married men with children, road roomies and best buds for years—had pulled off a huge, multi-person trade that had nothing to do with baseball.

The pitchers exchanged wives...along with their kids, houses, dogs and probably a goldfish or two to be named later.

Even for the early 1970s—the unofficial tail end of the Swingin' '60s, after all, and a few years removed from Hollywood's 1969 ode to spouse-swapping, *Bob & Carol & Ted & Alice*—this was still scintillating, titillating news.

Which is why Peterson, then 31, and Kekich, 27, decided to go to the New York press with such a juicy story before it became an out-of-control public scandal. In a March 1973 interview with the *Daily News* that was splashed across the front page, Peterson made it a point to tell sportswriter Phil Pepe that he hoped "you won't make anything sordid out of this."

Kekich added that, "Unless people know the full details, it could turn out to be a nasty type thing. Don't say this was wife-swapping, because it wasn't. We didn't swap wives, we swapped lives."

The pitchers, in separate sitdowns with Pepe, took great pains to explain how such a thing could happen. Peterson, a former All-Star and 20-game winner in his eighth season with the Yankees, and Kekich, a back-end starter who had been traded to New York from the Dodgers in 1968, became fast friends. So, naturally, did their wives.

Then nature really took its course. As the couples

grew closer, Fritz found himself falling in love with Susanne Kekich. Mike and Marilyn Peterson, meanwhile, shared what Kekich described as a strong physical attraction. Eventually, Peterson, who had two young sons, moved in with Susanne. Kekich, father of two girls, went to live with Marilyn.

"There are degrees of love involved," Kekich said. "We all tried something with a common understanding. It was completely a four-way thing."

Unfortunately for Kekich, his side of the love square didn't last. He and Marilyn Peterson split soon after the swap, with Kekich blaming their strong personalities for their inability to get along.

It turned out to be more than just a fling for Peterson and Susanne Kekich. They eventually married and have remained together since.

But just months after the couples switched spouses, the new arrangement ended up causing a rift between the pitchers, with Kekich expressing his bitterness to *The News* that he'd lost Susanne to his former friend and had nothing to show for it.

Yet both men insisted that the team came first and their off-the-field problems wouldn't be an issue in the clubhouse.

"In here, we're still teammates," Kekich said. "I suppose I'm fortunate in being able to disassociate myself from other things. When I play baseball, I play baseball, with nothing else on my mind.

"There's only one way to play baseball and the way to play baseball is as a team," he added.

"I'll be rooting for Mike when he's pitching," Peterson said. "I hope he wins 20 games this year. I hope I win 20. I hope all our pitchers win 20."

Being part of the freaky foursome apparently took a toll on the two pitchers, who both came nowhere near winning 20 games that season. Peterson, who for several years made a formidable one-two punch at the top of the rotation with ace Mel Stottlemyre, was coming off a 17-win season in 1972 and had won 81 games over the past five seasons for mostly bad to mediocre Yankee teams.

But Peterson had his worst season with the Bombers in '73, going 8-15 with a 3.95 ERA. The following year he was traded to the Cleveland Indians in a six-player deal that brought first baseman Chris Chambliss and starter-reliever Dick Tidrow to New York, who would become vital cogs in the team's late '70s reign.

Though the Yankees had vowed not to trade either pitcher despite all the negative attention, the front office seemingly used a poor start by Kekich in 1973—1-1 with a 9.20 ERA in four starts—as an excuse to cut ties.

Barely three months after he and Peterson went public with their news, Kekich was shipped off to Cleveland for a pitcher who never played a game for the Yankees. Kekich would bounce around the Majors, Japan and Mexico for the next four years and be out of the game by 32, as unlucky at baseball as he had been at love.

# Chapter Eight
## Graig Nettles' Superballs

When New York acquired Graig Nettles in a 1973 trade with the Cleveland Indians for a handful of bench warmers, it was the first big step in solidifying a mediocre lineup that would turn the post-Mickey Mantle Yankees into legitimate contenders and eventual two-time champions in the late '70s.

Nettles, a Gold Glove-caliber third baseman with a lefty power stroke perfectly suited for the Stadium, would lead the AL in 1976 with 32 home runs and would retire in 1988 with a total of 390 and the record for the most HR as a third baseman (319). A character known for his quick, biting wit as much as his quick, lethal bat, "Puff" would man the hot corner for 11 years and be a major contributor to the Yankees' four pennants and two World Series wins from 1976 to 1981.

Considering his power numbers weren't padded by PEDs, Nettles is arguably the best third-baseman in Yankees history not named A-Rod.

Then again, much like A-Fraud, Nettles was caught adding a little extra "bounce" to his sweet southpaw swing early in his Yankees career.

On Sept. 7, 1974, with the Yankees holding a slim,

one-game lead over both the Red Sox and Orioles, Nettles had already enjoyed a big day when he stepped up to the plate late in the nightcap of an important doubleheader against the Detroit Tigers.

Nettles, who had slugged a home run in the first game and another in the second for a 1-0 Yankees lead, this time hit a bloop, opposite-field single off the end of the bat that immediately touched off a commotion around home plate.

The top of the bat had shattered on impact with the pitch, sending shards of wood flying everywhere—along with what looked suspiciously like pieces of rubber.

Nettles had apparently "corked" his bat, a baseball no-no that entails drilling into the business end of a bat and filling the space with cork, sawdust—or, in Nettles' case, rubber—in order to lighten it and quicken a hitter's swing.

According to newspaper accounts of the day, it was a surreal scene around the plate, with superballs bouncing all over the grass and Tigers catcher Bill Freehan scrambling after them to collect as evidence for the umpires.

Nettles may have been embarrassed, but he was hardly contrite.

"I didn't know there was anything wrong with the bat," the slugger told reporters after the game.

"That was the first time I used it. Some Yankees fan in Chicago gave it to me and said it would bring me good luck. There's no brand name on it or anything. Maybe the guy made it himself. It had been in the bat rack and I picked it up by mistake, because it looked like the bat I had been using the last few days," added a straight-faced Nettles as reporters snickered.

The umpires were not amused, however. Nettles

was called out on the single, though his home run early in the game was allowed, giving the Yankees a much-needed 1-0 win and a 1.5-game lead in a tight pennant race they would eventually lose.

# Chapter Nine
**Mattingly's Mullet**

As if the Yankees didn't have enough to worry about after a rare and humiliating last-place finish in 1990, the following season was notable for a hairy situation that overshadowed the team's woeful lack of hitting, pitching, defense and morale.

It was the sorry spectacle of the Yankee front office—i.e., George Steinbrenner—alienating and embarrassing one of the more beloved Yankees of all time … over his hairstyle.

Despite his never having tasted World Series bubbly, few Yankees are as revered, respected and enduringly popular as Don Mattingly, the slick-fielding hit machine whose Hall of Fame-bound career was derailed by a back problem that sapped him of his power and forced him into early retirement just as the Bombers were at the cusp of their late-1990s dynasty.

Save for the dark decade of 1965 to 1975, when the team went through its first prolonged World Series drought, every Yankee era has been personified by its biggest star, starting with Babe Ruth and continuing through to Derek Jeter.

Mattingly, though, is the face of franchise

futility—and undoubtedly the unluckiest Yankee superstar ever. He had the misfortune of joining the team one season after their 1981 World Series appearance against the Los Angeles Dodgers and then retiring from a 13-year career in 1995, one season shy of the Yankees' first of four championships in five seasons.

When he came up for good in 1983, winning the American League batting title in his first full season and blossoming into the best all-around player in the game, no one could have foreseen that the first baseman's career would be divided into two disparate halves: six years of Lou Gehrig-like greatness followed by six years of Chris Chambliss steadiness after Mattingly never fully recovered from his back.

Worse yet, the Yankees were the winningest team in baseball during the 1980s, when Mattingly—a.k.a. Donnie Baseball to a generation of adoring fans—was in his prime.

But until the wild card was established—allowing the second-place Yankees to sneak into the playoffs in 1995, Mattingly's first and only postseason—the closest they came to an AL East title during his tenure was in 1985, when the Yanks won 97 games but blew a chance to overtake the Toronto Blue Jays on the final weekend of the season.

It may be easy to feel sorry for Mattingly, but he still owns one of the greatest of all Yankee careers, which includes a batting title, MVP award, nine Gold Gloves, several team records and a spectacular swan-song performance in the '95 division playoff series against the Seattle Mariners.

Not to mention having the rare honor of being

named captain in 1991, the tenth in Yankees history. Unfortunately, it was the same year that saw a disgusted Mattingly, already demoralized over being part of one of the worst Yankee teams ever, engage in a public pissing match with then-GM Gene Michael, get fined and punished with a one-game suspension.

All for the unpardonable Yankee sin of growing his hair too long.

The Yankees have long been known for their corporate, buttoned-up persona that includes a ban on long hair and beards, but Steinbrenner took it to the extreme. One of his first acts as managing general partner after buying the team in 1973 was to jot down the uniform numbers of players that needed a haircut (a list manager Ralph Houk is said to have promptly tossed in the garbage).

A hirsute Yankee captain breaking the team's grooming code was not without precedent. In 1977, Thurman Munson mischievously fanned one of the many fires that broke out between the tempestuous trinity of Steinbrenner, Billy Martin and Reggie Jackson. The catcher tweaked the owner by growing a beard and refusing to shave for nearly two weeks, finally taking razor to chin to avoid having his friend Martin catch hell from Steinbrenner for losing control of the team.

On August 15, 1991, Steinbrenner was in the midst of his second suspension from baseball, this time for his dealings with gambler Howie Spira. But there was little doubt exactly who had issued an edict demanding Mattingly get a haircut even if the official Yankee line was that it came from Michael.

It was left to manager Stump Merrill to deliver

the news to the Yankee star, who was already unhappy over playing for a lousy, lifeless team with a dysfunctional front office—he had asked for a trade earlier in the year—and frustrated over having to adjust to being a glorified singles hitter after back surgery.

While some press accounts called Mattingly's rule-breaking coif a "mullet," it was nowhere near a Billy Ray Cyrus special, by all accounts just an inch or so past his collar. But combined with a thick mustache that would make a '70s porn star jealous, Mattingly's appearance was considered unbecoming of a Yankee, let alone a Yankee captain, and Merrill ordered him, as well as three other Yankees, to get his locks lopped.

Mattingly's refusal touched off a war of words in the press between the general manager and his star player, with Merrill, already viewed as a company stooge by many of his players, caught in the middle.

"If someone from management tells you you need a haircut, you get a haircut," Merrill said.

"He's the captain and he's got a big contract. If we asked the captain to get his hair cut, he should get it cut," Michael said.

For his part, Mattingly used the incident to reveal for the first time that he had asked for a trade, adding, "Maybe this is their way of saying, 'We don't need you anymore.' "

Mattingly's teammates were equally disgusted, with DH Kevin Maas saying the whole affair was "so dumb," he didn't want to address it, and second-baseman Steve Sax calling it "nickel and dime."

"Somebody's hair," said Sax, "is a ridiculous way to tear down a team."

Mattingly's teammates may have rallied 'round their captain, but the effort didn't exactly translate onto the field. Mattingly, suspended one game, eventually got his hair trimmed and returned to the lineup. But the team, already coming off their first finish in the basement in 25 years, continued their downward spiral in 1991. The Yankees ended up in fifth place, 20 games under .500 at 71-91.

For Merrill, it was a case of hair today, gone that winter. The Yankees' third losing season in row, the second with Merrill at the helm, cost the befuddled skipper his job.

# Chapter Ten
## The Whiz Kids of '85

Of all the things one can get arrested for, relieving yourself behind a dumpster in a Kansas City shopping mall doesn't exactly rate as a crime against humanity.

But when you're one of baseball's rising young stars, the reigning American League batting champion and the most popular player on the New York Yankees, taking a whiz in public is a pretty pee-brained idea.

Especially if you get caught.

Long before Don Mattingly ran afoul of Yankee law by growing his hair too long, the first baseman was busted by Kansas City authorities on a charge of indecent conduct—an ominous way of saying he took a leak outside.

On the evening of May 9, 1985, with the team in town for a three-game set against the Royals, Mattingly was hanging out at a restaurant located in Kansas City's Country Club Plaza, a snazzy shopping center known for its high-end stores.

Mattingly, who would later swear he wasn't drunk, left the joint near midnight and apparently couldn't hold it in any longer. He was nabbed in the act by a Plaza guard, hauled to the security office and issued a municipal summons for indecent conduct in public.

A baseball player getting arrested no matter how trivial the charge would normally be big news, never mind that it was Mattingly, already a big Yankee name at 24.

Yet the story didn't leak out for several days—and only after another Yankee, infielder Dale Berra, was also busted in Kansas City three days later.

For urinating in public.

After leaving the same restaurant as Mattingly.

By the same security guard.

Berra, the 28-year-old son of Yankee legend Yogi Berra, had been traded to New York the previous winter from the Pittsburgh Pirates in a low-level deal widely seen as a front office favor to Yogi, who was the Bombers' skipper for all of 1984 and going into 1985—not a small feat in a decade marked by George Steinbrenner's penchant for playing musical chairs with his managers.

While the Yankees succeeded in hiding Mattingly's arrest from the public for a while, the game was up after Berra was caught doing his business in a Plaza parking garage. But instead of quietly accepting a municipal summons like Mattingly, Berra pushed the security officer, according to a police report, resisted attempts to be handcuffed and then made matters worse by taking a swing at the guard.

With assault added to the indecent conduct charge, it didn't take long for both players' arrests to go public. Berra's charges were misdemeanors, but they carried a maximum penalty of six months in jail and a $500 fine.

Though the Yankees initially denied Mattingly had been charged with anything,
the floodgates soon opened, so to speak, on what would become a highly embarrassing episode for the players and the team.

A *Daily News* headline said it best: "Whiz Kids," a sly nod to the 1950s Philadelphia Phillies' nickname that obviously took on a whole new meaning here.

It also turned out that the restaurant both players had frequented happened to be co-owned by then-Yankee hitting coach Lou Piniella, who likely wasn't too sweet on the kind of publicity his joint was getting.

Even worse: They had pissed off George Steinbrenner, who fined each of them $1,000.

"I'm convinced it's embarrassing to these two young men," said the Boss, clearly meaning it was an embarrassment to him and all things Yankee. "They're dead wrong."

The Whiz Kids tried to downplay their antics, each copping to their respective "mistake" as they faced court hearings back in Kansas City that season.

"I went behind a dumpster. I wasn't drunk or anything like that, but it was stupid," Mattingly said. "It was a mistake, not a bad mistake, but a mistake. I was wrong. I learned my lesson. I'll pay my fine and I won't do it again."

"I made a mistake, as minor as it was," echoed Berra, seemingly oblivious to the assault charge. "But I will gladly pay the fine."

The charges were eventually dropped for both players, but Berra's arrest was just the latest incident in what turned out to be a rough year for him.

His father had pretty much handed him the

regular shortstop job at the beginning of the 1985 season. But when the Yankees started off 6-10, an impatient Steinbrenner canned Yogi and installed Billy Martin as manager for a third time.

Berra was actually hitting over .300 when Martin—an old pal of Yogi's whom Dale thought of as an uncle—benched him for good.

He may have been the son of baseball's most beloved ambassador, but Berra was no angel. Later that year, he would besmirch the family name when he admitted to cocaine use during testimony at the so-called Pittsburgh Drug Trials that outed several big leaguers as cokeheads, the game's biggest black eye since the 1919 Black Sox fix.

Berra, released by the Yankees the following year, couldn't shake his drug problem. In 1989, two years after his career ended at age 30 with the Houston Astros (where Yogi was now a coach), he was charged with cocaine possession. The charges were later dismissed, and Yogi's wayward son has reportedly been living the sober life ever since.

For Mattingly, what happened in Kansas City in 1985 pretty much stayed there, the natural result of having a tremendous year and becoming the face of the Yankees.

With new Yankee Rickey Henderson constantly on base in front of him and Dave Winfield batting behind him, Donnie Baseball enjoyed his finest season. His 35 HR, 145 RBI, .324 campaign saw him win his only MVP award and the first of nine Gold Gloves, making his misadventure behind a dumpster just a minor stain on an otherwise great year.

# Chapter Eleven
## Luis Polonia's Bad Math

Based on his solid 12-year career in the Major Leagues, the scouting report on Luis Polonia would read something like this:

Good contact hitter with excellent speed; below-average outfielder with weak arm; has trouble keeping track of a count.

That last one, by the way, does not refer to balls and strikes.

Midway through the 1989 season, when the Yankees finally got tired of Rickey Henderson's selfishness and eccentricities and traded him back to the Oakland A's for three players, the one they were most excited to get in return was Polonia, a young, top-of-the-order speedster who could hit for average and hopefully fill most of the void left by Henderson's departure.

But less than two months after Polonia put on the pinstripes, the Yankees were probably thinking Henderson's daily diva act wasn't so bad after all.

On the morning of August 16, during a series against the Brewers in Milwaukee, Polonia was arrested after cops found a 15-year-old girl in his room at the Pfister Hotel who was presumably there for more than the outfielder's autograph.

The girl, who met Polonia at the Brewers' County Stadium during the game the night before, had been reported missing when she never came home. Friends told her mother she was meeting the Dominican-born player, then 24 years old and in his third year in the Majors, and cops headed straight to Polonia's room at the Pfister, where the Yankees always stayed when in town.

Polonia, who would later be found guilty of having sex with a minor and serve 27 days of a 60-day jail sentence after the season, at first figured he had a great defense.

"All I know, to this day, is she said she was 19," Polonia told the *New York Daily News* years later. "When she said that, I thought there was no problem. I didn't know her. She seemed like a pretty nice girl."

Yankees owner George Steinbrenner, who always had a soft spot for troubled players, even those bad at math, went to bat for Polonia during the trial, telling the judge he was just "a little kid who really doesn't know his way around."

The team got rid of Polonia the following April anyway, trading him to the California Angels, where he hit .336. But the Yankees, who always liked his lefty bat and speed, would eventually forgive Polonia for his embarrassing indiscretion.

He was welcomed back to the Bronx in 1994, hitting .311 and stealing 20 bases in a strike-shortened season, and then had a third stint with the Yankees in 2000. Coming off the bench for the squad that beat the Mets in the World Series, and older and wiser Polonia hit .286 and had presumably learned to check IDs.

# Chapter Twelve
## The Highs and Lows of Mark Whiten

If ever there was a ballplayer who experienced both the dizzying highs and depressing lows of a major league career, it was Marc Whiten, a journeyman outfielder who managed to join two exclusive clubs on opposite ends of the baseball spectrum over an otherwise mediocre career.

Whiten, a switch-hitter who played for nine teams in an 11-year span from 1990 to 2000, is just one of a handful of ballplayers to hit four home runs in one game.

He's also one of a select group of players to be arrested for sexual assault, an embarrassing episode that occurred while he was a member of the Yankees.

On September 7, 1993, in his first of two seasons with the St. Louis Cardinals, Whiten had a pretty good week in one night. In the second game of a home twin bill against the Cincinnati Reds, he went deep four times, carrying the Cards to a 15-2 win. The feat tied a record held by nine players at the time (four more have done it since), including such immortals as Lou Gehrig, Willie Mays and Mike Schmidt.

Whiten spread the damage around, connecting off of three pitchers on a first-inning grand slam, a pair of three-run homers and a two-run shot in the ninth.

He also knocked in 12 runs that game, tying yet another all-time record set in 1924 by Cardinals' Hall of Fame slugger Jim Bottomley, who drove in a dozen in a game against the Brooklyn Dodgers.

Whiten's four-for-five for the ages capped off what would be his best year ever—25 HR, 99 RBI, .253—but he would never come close to that kind of production again.

Four years and another four teams later, Whiten, then 30, had developed a reputation as an inconsistent cipher who would never live up to his potential. Yet he scored a one-year, $1 million contract with the Yankees as a free agent before the 1997 season, and appeared in 69 games as a spare outfielder for the defending world champions.

His five HR, 24 RBI season would have been just a forgotten footnote in Yankee history if not for what did—or didn't—transpire in the wee hours of a hot Milwaukee morning in the midst of a weekend series against the Brewers.

Before dawn on Saturday, July 19, Milwaukee cops were called about an "incident" at the hotel where the Yankees were staying—the infamous Pfister, which held bad karma for the Yankees throughout their history as the site of Rick Dempsey's lobby beatdown of Bill Sudakis in 1975 and Luis Polonia's illicit liaison with an underaged girl in 1989.

Police were investigating a complaint from a 31-year-old Wisconsin woman who, according to cops and an unidentified Yankee player, had accompanied Whiten to his room after Friday night's game.

Whiten, though, wasn't arrested until Monday, after police finally concluded a sexual assault "might have occurred." Whiten, who insisted the sex was consensual, was released on a $10,000 bond.

The scandal couldn't have come at a worse time for both Whiten and the Yankees, who were already short on outfielders and middle-of-the-order power thanks to injuries.

But it was especially bad timing for Whiten. Though never formally charged by Milwaukee police, his particular peccadillo set him apart from a growing list of pro athletes who have found themselves in similar situations.

Not only was Whiten married, his wife had given birth to the couple's second child just two days before the alleged assault took place. Whiten, in fact, had been cleared by Torre to see his new son in Florida and had rejoined the team before Friday's game.

No surprise then, that Whiten was greeted with a chorus of boos in his first game back at Yankee Stadium after his arrest. Asked about the fans' reaction, the disgraced outfielder unwittingly summed up his own career when he said: "It's been hard, yeah. But you have to take the good with the bad and just move on."

Whiten moved on soon after—the Yankees, despite being decimated by injuries, released him in mid-August about three weeks after the scandal. It didn't help Whiten's cause that he had already gotten on George Steinbrenner's bad side earlier that season when it was revealed Whiten had been hanging out with pitcher Dwight Gooden in an Arlington, Texas, strip club on the night Gooden got into an ugly brawl with a cabdriver.

Whiten was eventually cleared when prosecutors

decided not to press charges due to lack of evidence. He would continue his journeyman ways south of the border, playing in a Mexican league before signing in 1998 with the Cleveland Indians, where he would end his once-promising career two years later at 33.

## Chapter Thirteen
**The Yankee Flipper**

After having their collective hearts broken in the strike-shortened season of 1994, Yankee fans hungry for a title welcomed former Cy Young winner Jack McDowell to the Bronx with open arms.

The righty reciprocated by giving them the finger.

McDowell wasn't even 29 years old yet when the suddenly resurgent Yankees pulled off a huge trade in the winter of '94, acquiring the Chicago White Sox ace for a pair of no-name minor leaguers in the hopes "Black Jack" would anchor a young pitching staff and help put the team over the top after a players' strike had effectively canceled the last two months of the season—including the World Series—with the Bombers comfortably in first place and seemingly headed to their first postseason since 1981.

He may have been regarded as a free spirit and a bit of a flake thanks mostly to his off-season job—playing guitar in a rock band—but McDowell was rock-solid on the mound. He was an old-school workhorse who averaged about 250 innings a year and twice led the American League in complete games as a member of the White Sox.

Before playing for the Yankees in 1995, his one and only season in pinstripes, he was already a three-time All-Star and a two-time 20-game winner, including his Cy Young year in 1993 when he went 22-10 with a 3.37 ERA.

And so it was with great expectations that this would finally be the Yankees' year—despite the veteran joining a staff that included unproven, if promising homegrown southpaws Sterling Hitchcock and rookie Andy Pettitte, plus a skinny spot starter-reliever from Panama named Mariano Rivera.

McDowell, though, didn't exactly bring his first-rate stuff from the Second City. By July 18, more than halfway into the season, the lackluster Yankees were mired in fourth place in the A.L. East at 33-38, six games behind the division-leading Boston Red Sox.

Black Jack, who as the highest-paid Yankee that year was making more than $5 million per, had only seven wins and an ERA approaching 4.50 when he took the mound in the nightcap of a doubleheader at the Stadium against his old White Sox team.

Frustrated New York fans, who had already witnessed their team get battered in the opener, 9-4, watched helplessly as the alleged ace got tagged by his former mates for nine runs and 13 hits by the fifth inning.

Trudging back to the dugout with his head down after being pulled by manager Buck Showalter, McDowell was unceremoniously serenaded by the boo-birds in attendance.

The pitcher responded by raising his arm and giving the Stadium faithful a single-finger salute.

With that taboo gesture, the ever-clever tabloids

bestowed on Black Jack a new Yankee nickname for the ages: The Yankee Flipper.

McDowell undoubtedly won over some born n' bred New Yorkers in the crowd who appreciated his chutzpah—years earlier, beloved catcher Thurman Munson had himself flipped Stadium boo-birds the bird after during a bad game, and was roundly cheered in his next at-bat.

But the Yankee front office wasn't amused by McDowell, nor was the New York media. The team fined McDowell $5,000, while a *New York Times* headline blared: "Trade him!"

"Obviously I wish I had it back," McDowell said. "It's frustrating to get hit like that, then you realize that everybody realizes you were as bad as you are."

Asked whether he needed to win back any sensitive souls he may have offended, McDowell replied honestly. "Not really. I don't need to win anybody back. I need to win games."

That's pretty much what McDowell did the rest of the year, as the Yankees clawed back into the race with a fury, clinching the first-ever American League wild card on the final day of the regular season.

McDowell helped lead the charge. He ended up leading the team in wins, with 15, as well as shutouts (2), complete games (8), strikeouts (157) and innings pitched (217), and winning back fans in the process.

His redemption, unfortunately, didn't last long.

In the thrilling division series against the Seattle Mariners, the Yankees were up two games to none in the best-of-five matchup when Black Jack lost Game 3, the potential clincher.

The worst was still to come.

*Robert Dominguez & David Hinckley*

In a relief appearance late in Game 5, McDowell coughed up the lead—and the win—by giving up a walk-off, two-run double to Ken Griffey Jr. in the bottom of the 12th that sent the Yankees home early in their first postseason in 14 years.

Heartbroken Yankee fans watching at home responded by giving the Yankee Flipper a one-fingered salute of their own.

## Chapter Fourteen
### The Case of the Missing Mitt

He was supposed to be the next Mickey Mantle, a five-tool outfielder who also happened to be the younger cousin of Yankee legend Mariano Rivera.

Instead, Ruben Rivera will forever be remembered in Bomber lore as the failed prospect who committed baseball's ultimate cardinal sin.

Thou shalt not steal from a teammate.

Especially when that teammate is a Yankee god named Derek Jeter.

Unlike his cousin Mariano, who struggled as a starter before finding his niche as a reliever, Ruben Rivera was a highly-touted, can't-miss prospect when he made the big club as a September call-up in 1995, a strapping 21-year-old from Panama who was being groomed to be the next homegrown Yankee star to patrol the hallowed ground in centerfield for years.

In 1995, Baseball America ranked him as the No. 2 prospect in the nation, just behind Alex Rodriguez and in front of No. 3 Chipper Jones and Jeter at No. 4. Didn't happen. Unlike his cousin Mariano—a team-first, humble man who set an example on and off the field—Rivera was an undisciplined, immature player who drove management crazy with his antics on and off the field.

It wasn't just a reputation for being a late-night carouser. Playing for the Yanks' Triple-A Columbus team in 1995, Rivera was benched by then-manager Stump Merrill for being constantly late to games. Rivera left the ballpark in a huff, cleaning out his locker and earning a seven-game suspension in the process.

As a rookie in 1996, Rivera saw limited action in the ALDS against the Texas Rangers, striking out in his only at bat. But he certainly made an impression with the veterans that postseason. Rivera's companion on one of the team's charter flights was a 17-year-old hot dog vendor he'd met at Yankee Stadium, who boarded the flight in less-than-appropriate attire that offended the other players' wives and girlfriends.

The following spring, doctors diagnosed a strain in Rivera's right shoulder presumably caused by showing off his throwing arm the previous September, when Rivera uncorked two strong, but unnecessary throws from right field in a 19-2 blowout of the Milwaukee Brewers. The injury, which would put Rivera on the shelf for the first few months of the season, meant the team would be short on outfielders.

Ever the diplomat, manager Joe Torre chalked the throws up to youthful exuberance, while still calling it "a foolish thing to do." But despite Rivera's potential, the Yankees had seen enough. The team sent the strikeout-prone player to the San Diego Padres in April in a deal that brought Japanese pitcher Hideki Irabu to the Bronx.

Getting away from the pressure of playing for the Yankees didn't do a thing for Rivera. In four years with the Padres, he hit only .204 in 1,026 at-bats, striking out an astounding 341 times—a .332 strikeout average, as it were, or once every three at-bats.

By comparison, another Yankee outfielder, a fellow by the name of Joe DiMaggio, struck out 369 times over a 13-year career.

After being released by San Diego and having a lackluster 2001 season with the Cincinnati Reds, Rivera, now 28, found himself back with the Yankees at the start of spring training in 2002, armed with a $1,000,000-a-year free agent contract and dreams of finally putting it all together with the team that had invested so much hope in his talent.

Nope, didn't happen. Rather than blossom, an older but hardly wiser Rivera hit bottom. Barely a month into spring training, the former phenom was booted off the team after stealing a glove and bat from Jeter's locker (Rivera may have also taken a glove belonging to first baseman Jason Giambi).

Incredibly, Rivera, who was lucky to be back with the Yankees, let alone pulling down a million bucks a years, put his career and reputation on the line for what amounted to a couple of weeks worth of meal money.

Rivera had peddled Jeter's glove to a memorabilia collector for $2,500.

Clubhouse justice was swift. Despite an embarrassed Rivera having returned the items—and a mortified Mariano Rivera going to bat for his kid cousin—Ruben was essentially voted off the Yankees by teammates and coaches alike.

"The clubhouse is a special place," Torre said. "It's our sanctuary. "It's big part of what we do. Trust is very important."

Rivera tried to downplay his actions, telling a Panama news station he had made a "rookie's error"—though he was 28 and about to start his eighth Major League season.

"I didn't kill anyone," he said. "I did it without thinking, because it wasn't for the money. I had a good contract. It was just an instant when I wasn't thinking, and I made a mistake that I'm paying for now."

Released by the Yankees—albeit with $200,000 in walking-away money—Rivera spent the next two seasons as a part-timer with the Texas Rangers and San Francisco Giants, never hitting above .209.

He was out of baseball by 30, a seemingly sad end to a career that once held so much promise.

Except Rivera found redemption of sorts—south of the border. He became the Mickey Mantle of the Mexican League, a perennial .300 hitter with speed who averaged more than 20 home runs a season.

In 2014, at the age of 40, Rivera was the centerfielder for the Rieleros de Aguascalientes—the Mexican League champions as recently as 2012—and presumably staying away from teammates' lockers.

# Chapter Fifteen
## Michael Pineda's Sticky Situation

The Yankees waited a long time to reap the fruits of their controversial 2012 trade for pitcher Miguel Pineda, and when the strapping, 6'7" righty finally made his Yankee debut two years later after a raft of injuries, it looked like New York had itself a future ace in the making.

That is, until Pineda got caught with his hand—and neck—in the pine-tar jar.

Pineda was 23 and coming off a solid rookie season in 2011 for the Mariners, one that included a selection to the All-Star game when the Yankees traded power-hitting catching prospect Jesus Montero for him in January 2012.

Despite Pineda's upside, the deal enraged some Yankees fans who saw Montero as the second coming of Jorge Posada. It certainly didn't help that Pineda seemed like damaged goods right off the bat. He went on the disabled list with tendinitis in spring training and then suffered a tear in his shoulder that kept him off a Major League mound all through the 2012 and 2013 seasons.

Making matters worse, Pineda's maturity was

called into question when he was charged with driving under the influence while rehabbing in Tampa.

But Pineda managed to silence the naysayers, at least temporarily, at the start of the 2014 season. Finally healthy and tabbed as the No. 5 starter, the hard-throwing Dominican Republic native made an impressive debut as a Yankee, dominating the Toronto Blue Jays through six strong innings in which he gave up one run on five hits and notched five strikeouts.

He followed that up a week later with an even better performance. In his Yankee Stadium coming-out against the hated Red Sox, Pineda gave up one run and struck out seven in six innings, picking up his first win in pinstripes and giving Yankee faithful reason to think the team may have gotten the better of that 2012 deal, after all. Montero, once considered a can't-miss prospect, had so far been a bust for the Mariners.

Pineda's first taste of Yankee victory, however, was bittersweet. TV cameras clearly showed a brown, shiny substance on his pitching hand that Boston announcers were quick to identify as pine tar, the sticky stuff hitters use to get a better grip on their bats but is forbidden to be used by pitchers because it can alter the flight of the ball.

The Red Sox, who could have easily brought the alleged cheating to the attention of the umps, remained surprisingly mum—cynical minds figured it was because two top Boston pitchers, Jon Lester and Clay Bucholz, were widely suspected of doctoring balls, too.

After the game, Pineda told reporters the brown stuff was nothing but dirt because his hands "get sweaty," he explained. "I don't use pine tar."

Still, Major League officials quietly warned the Yankees to keep Pineda on the up-and-up, and the matter was dropped and the mystery remained unsolved.

Until Pineda's next start, also against the Red Sox.

In the second inning, Boston manager John Farrell bounded out of the dugout to ask the umps to check Pineda. He had no choice: Hi-def cameras had once again detected a brown substance on Pineda— except this time the pitcher had slathered it on the side of his neck in a lame attempt to conceal the pine tar against his dark skin.

Considering it was a cool April night in Boston, a sheepish Pineda couldn't blame sweaty hands this time for wanting to get a better grip on the baseball.

"It was cold, I couldn't feel the ball in the first inning, I didn't want to hit nobody," Pineda offered. "I apologize to my teammates, and to everybody.

"I'll learn from this mistake. It won't happen again," added the pitcher, who earned himself a 10-game suspension and special recognition in the Yankees' Bad-Boy Hall of Shame for Dopiest Cheating Attempt Ever.

# Part II
## BRAWLS

# Chapter Sixteen
## The Battle of the Biltmore

To say George Steinbrenner had his faults as an owner is a lot like saying Billy Martin was fond of engaging in a spirited debate after a cocktail or two.

But no matter how irrational, irascible or irresponsible those two could be, they can't hold a candle to Larry MacPhail, the Yankee co-owner and front office executive whose Hall of Fame career imploded during a spectacular public flameout that would come to be known as "The Battle of the Biltmore."

MacPhail, a banker's son from Michigan, was by all accounts a hard-drinking, difficult, colorful character prone to outlandish, erratic behavior. Though his affinity for alcohol had more than a little to do with some of his infamous antics—like the night he and his equally booze-addled Red Sox counterpart Tom Yawkey traded Joe DiMaggio for Ted Williams before coming to their senses—MacPhail would come to be widely considered a visionary and innovator who helped modernize the game in the mid-20th century.

A lawyer by trade, MacPhail began his baseball career as part-owner of a St. Louis Cardinals minor league team in Columbus, Ohio, where he learned enough about running a baseball team to be named president and general manager of the Cincinnati Reds in 1933.

He would soon move on to the Dodgers in the same capacity, where his frequent spats with manager Leo Durocher made the daily drama of the "George & Billy Show" look like a church play.

Leo the Lip, no shrinking violet himself, probably underestimated the number of times he'd been fired by MacPhail—at least 60, according to Durocher's autobiography, *Nice Guys Finish Last*—only to be rehired in the morning once MacPhail was no longer in his cups.

Durocher, who once shoved MacPhail to the floor during one of their countless arguments—only to have a tearful MacPhail get up and hug him, according to Durocher—considered his mercurial boss to be "half madman, half genius."

"There is that thin line between genius and insanity, and in Larry's case it was sometimes so thin that you could see him drifting back and forth," Durocher wrote. "They always said this about MacPhail: Cold sober he was brilliant. One drink and he was even more brilliant. Two drinks—that's another story."

Decades before Steinbrenner's bizarro behavior would become comedy fodder for the likes of "Seinfeld," MacPhail was out-George-ing George. Like the Boss, MacPhail was prone to terrorizing subordinates, firing and often rehiring them on a whim.

He once canned his son's fiancé, who worked in

the Dodger front office, for letting MacPhail's estranged wife room with her.

The Roaring Redhead was also prone to second-guessing his managers, a habit that drove Durocher crazy but would drive away two iconic Yankees in one year.

In 1945, the triumvirate of MacPhail, Del Webb and Dan Topping purchased the Yankees, with MacPhail assuming general manager duties like he had done in Brooklyn and Cincinnati.

The new owners kept ol' Joe McCarthy, still the winningest skipper in team history and the proud owner of seven World Series rings. But McCarthy resigned barely two months into the 1946 season because of "health" issues—in essence, he was sick and damn tired of MacPhail's constant meddling.

Bill Dickey, the Hall of Fame catcher who became player-manager after McCarthy's resignation, quit in mid-September due to the constant headache of working under MacPhail. Coach Johnny Neun, who took the helm for the remainder of the '46 season, was the team's third pilot that year, a foreshadowing of the managerial musical chairs played under Steinbrenner's reign.

The Yankees' lot improved considerably the next year. Under new manager Bucky Harris—the fourth in three years under McPhail & Co., if you're counting—the Bombers beat out the Red Sox for the AL pennant on the final weekend, then faced the Dodgers in a thrilling, seven-game Fall Classic best-known for Yankee pitcher Bill Bevens blowing a no-hitter in Game 5, Dodger outfielder Al Gionfriddo robbing Joe DiMaggio of a three-run homer in Game 6, and New

York reliever Joe Page hurling five shutout innings to seal Game 7 for the Bombers and give the team its first championship since the war year of 1943.

It only took MacPhail a few drunken minutes to ruin a season's worth of success.

As the jubilant Yankees celebrated their 11th championship in the Stadium clubhouse, MacPhail stormed in and stole the spotlight from the team and its rookie manager by announcing his retirement. Everyone was stunned; no one, especially the horde of New York reporters who'd grown accustomed to MacPhail's excesses since his Dodgers day, knew whether to take the unpredictable owner-GM seriously.

MacPhail wasn't finished. At the victory party in midtown Manhattan's staid Biltmore Hotel a little later, he was several more sheets into the wind when he summarily fired the Yanks' farm director, George Weiss—supposedly in front of his wife—and may have taken a swing at him, too, according to McPhail's son, Lee, who worked for the Yankees at the time.

Though no one saw it, MacPhail was said to have slugged his partner Topping while they were off somewhere arguing. For good measure, MacPhail definitely punched a reporter who had written something unflattering about the tempestuous GM—the poor scribe a former long-time aide of MacPhail's from his National League days.

MacPhail may have just been blowing smoke about quitting, but the Biltmore meltdown sealed his fate. His irate partners gave him until dawn to accept a buyout, and the Roaring Redhead faded away into Yankee history with a whimper, though $2 million richer.

It was a sad end to what was otherwise a brilliant baseball career. Among other things, MacPhail was the force behind night baseball, introducing it in 1935 at Cincinnati's Crosley Field, and he saw the value in broadcasting games on the radio when other owners were afraid it would bite into gate receipts (a move that introduced future Yankee announcer Red Barber to baseball).

Like Steinbrenner, MacPhail wasn't afraid to invest in his teams even as the Great Depression and World War II whittled attendance. He turned the Dodgers into a profitable club and a perennial contender by paying top dollar to sign good players and sprucing up Ebbets Field to lure Brooklyn's rabid fan base to the park.

MacPhail's other legacy: His son Lee and grandson Andy would also become successful baseball execs, with Lee joining his dad in the Hall of Fame as the only father-son duo in Cooperstown.

## Chapter Seventeen
### The Major vs. the Minor Pitcher

The Battle of the Biltmore in 1947 wouldn't be the last time Yankee personnel engaged in victory-party fisticuffs.

In 1958, pitcher Ryne Duren, a fireballing rookie reliever whose 20 saves and 2.02 ERA helped New York clinch the American League pennant by mid-September, made the mistake of picking a fight with Ralph Houk while the team held its clinching celebration aboard a train bound for Detroit.

With the exception of outfielder Hank Bauer, a Marine Corps lieutenant wounded in Okinawa, Houk was the last guy on the Yankees anyone would want to challenge. The former backup catcher-turned-coach, 39, was a grizzled, cigar-chomping, no-nonsense type affectionately known as the Major—his rank as a U.S. Army Ranger in World War II, where his combat heroics in campaigns like the Battle of the Bulge earned him a chest full of hardware that included a Silver Star and Purple Heart.

But late in the evening of September 14, 1958, after a long Sunday in which the Yanks had swept a doubleheader in Kansas City to guarantee their fourth straight World Series appearance, Duren lived up to his reputation as an out-of-control drunk.

Not content to revel in the fact he was a key cog on a pennant-winning team, he figured it'd be a grand idea to liven up the festivities by calling out the Major.

Duren was hardly a kid who didn't know how to handle his liquor. Though only in his first full year in the majors, he was already 29 years old. He had come to the Yankees the year before from the Kansas City Athletics in a six-player swap that, ironically enough had banished bad-boy Billy Martin to the K.C. sticks after the infamous Copacabana fight.

The Yankees, it seemed, had traded one hard-drinking headache for another despite Duren's emergence as the team's colorful, lights-out closer. The tall righty reputedly threw a 100 mph fastball—he just didn't always know where it was going.

Born with bad vision, he wore thick spectacles on the mound but turned his weakness into a shtick that supposedly scared the wits out of opposing batters. Upon entering a game, he'd blink in the general direction of home plate a few times, then throw his first blazing warm-up pitch way over the heads of the catcher, batter and ump.

The routine, in fact, would later serve as the inspiration for Charlie Sheen's Wild Thing character in the *Major League* films.

Sometimes that first wild warm-up would come in low, too.

"Hitters don't like to see that fella," Yankee manager Casey Stengel once said of Duren. "Especially family men."

Duren's teammates didn't particularly like to see

that fella when he was in his cups, either, which was apparently not an uncommon sight. He already had a bit of a history with Houk, who had managed him in the minors and had, according to a newspaper report, once "tamed [Duren] with his fists."

"Duren can't drink," Houk told the paper. "He's a Jekyll and Hyde."

The pitcher's dark side emerged on the overnight trek to Motor City. Apparently still peeved at the taming Houk gave him, a drunken Duren tried to get a rise out of the coach by baiting him verbally, trotting out an old schoolyard line that went something like, "You're not so tough."

Houk, calmly chewing on his cigar, chose to ignore him.

That is, until Duren proceeded to mash the Major's stogie into his face.

Accounts of what happened next vary—the Yankees, as well as the beat reporters who witnessed the altercation, kept it all hush-hush, as baseball writers for the most part did in that era. But it was generally agreed Houk once again tamed the unruly pitcher with his fists.

Except Duren didn't take it so easily this time. It took a handful of Yankees to finally get him settled down, but not before he managed to kick fellow pitcher Don Larsen in the mouth, drawing blood.

Duren got the worst of it, though. Houk, ten years older and three inches shorter than his opponent, opened a gash over Duren's eye during the melee, a deep wound likely caused by the thick World Series ring Houk sported.

"This shouldn't happen," said Stengel a few days

later, after details of the fight were made public by a New York paper that chose to break the taboo on such a juicy story.

"You get whiskey slick and then you fight with your own," added the disgusted manager, using one of his favorite euphemisms for drinking.

All was seemingly forgiven later that fall, when the Yankees took a thrilling Series against the Milwaukee Braves after being down three games to one. Duren handled himself well. Though he lost the opener in the tenth inning, he saved Game 3—a 4-0 gem from Larsen—and was the winning pitcher in Game 6 to force a deciding tilt.

No record exists of how hard Duren partied after the Game 7 win. Or how wide a berth he gave Houk during the celebration.

There is a happy ending: Duren, who would kick around the Majors for a few years with a succession of teams after the Yankees traded him during the 1961 season, eventually dried out and spent his life counseling other alcoholics until his death in 2011 at age 81.

# Chapter Eighteen
## The Copa Brawl

In case anyone doubts there's a difference between the *New York Times* and the New York tabloid press, consider the headlines that appeared on the front page of the *Times* and the *Daily News* on June 4, 1957.

*Times:* "Yanks Fine 6 Players $5,500 for Café Visit."

*Daily News*: "Yanks Bench 2 in Copa Brawl."

Both were accurate. *The Daily News* headline was truer.

Calling the events of May 15, 1957, at the Copacabana nightclub a "café visit" is like describing the annual Fourth of July Nathan's Hot Dog Eating Contest as "a luncheon."

Funny thing is, by many accounts of what went down that night, the Yankee players involved in the brawl—or, if you will, the visit—were more on the side of right than wrong.

It was still an ugly affair for the team, and for those keeping score at home, it triggered the first of Billy Martin's Yankee firings.

Things started with at least the veneer of innocence. On May 15, the eve of Martin's 29th birthday, a bunch of his pals took him out on the town to celebrate.

Those pals included Mickey Mantle, Hank Bauer, Whitey Ford, Yogi Berra and Johnny Kucks.

For the record, everyone but Martin was accompanied by his wife. His own wife. The idea was to hit some nightspots, which is how the party ended up at the Copacabana, which may not have been the hottest spot north of Havana, but was an important stop for important people.

The headliner that night was Sammy Davis Jr., then at his performance peak and a favorite among the sports crowd.

Well, some of the sports crowd. All the baseball players liked him, but apparently he wasn't so admired by a bowling club that had also come by for the show.

While reports on the precise chain of events were contradictory and often seemingly filtered through a few drinks, there was some consensus that members of the bowling club were heckling Davis, and the verbal mix included racial epithets.

There's no dispute that a confrontation ensued and that Edward Jones, a bowler whose day job was running a deli in the Bronx, ended up with a broken jaw.

Jones fingered Bauer as the perp and when the police arrived, he demanded Bauer be arrested for slugging him.

Police declined, and on May 21 Jones had Bauer taken into custody on a citizen's arrest.

Bauer denied he had hit Jones, and he was never convicted. Nor were any of the others.

For media purposes, the story was still a delicious gift—which makes it almost defy belief that the papers didn't find out about it until 19 days after it happened.

*Robert Dominguez & David Hinckley*

They might not have found out then except that on June 3, the Yankees fined the six players—essentially for embarrassing the team. Yankee President George Weiss had worked hard to portray his players as moral paragons of impeccable character, and at the very least this tarnished that brand.

Mantle and Berra, who made $62,000 and $60,000 respectively, were fined $1,000 each—the equivalent of about $100,000 for a setup reliever earning $6 million in 2014.

Ford ($35,000 salary), Bauer ($27,500) and Martin ($21,000) were also fined $1,000 each. Kucks, whose shutout victory in game seven of the 1956 World Series had earned him a $15,000 salary for 1957, was fined $500.

Manager Casey Stengel later said he was irritated that his players were out carousing the night before a game.

But Casey also was from the school that believed punishing a player really punishes the team, so he saw no reason to impose any drastic on-the-field sanctions. His discipline consisted of dropping Bauer temporarily to the eighth spot in the lineup and blaming the media.

"This all happened three weeks ago," he said. "They're trying to make a big scandal of this because we're the Yanks."

Well, maybe. But having the town's best-known sports celebrities throwing punches in a high-profile Manhattan nightspot was the kind of story that tended to sell itself.

There was speculation in subsequent years that the straight-laced Weiss was uncomfortable with the shrug-it-off response of Casey, who in his own career was not always known as a player who went straight to his room at night and read the letters of St. Paul to the Ephesians.

Three years later, Weiss would fire a surprised and angry Stengel after the Yankees lost the 1960 World Series to the Pittsburgh Pirates.

Whatever the drama between Weiss and Stengel, the aftermath of the brawl did confirm that Weiss considered Martin a bad influence on Mantle—as if Mickey needed bad influences to do whatever he felt like doing.

A month later, Martin and Ralph Terry were traded to Kansas City, then for all practical purposes a Yankees farm team, for Suitcase Simpson and Ryne Duren.

As for the fines, Berra was philosophical.

At least," he said, "I can deduct it from my income taxes."

## Chapter Nineteen
### The Battle of the Pfister

Two years before the Yankees finally reached the World Series in 1976 after a 12-year post-season drought, the team's slim hopes for a division title were inadvertently dashed by a berserk backup catcher who went ballistic in the lobby of a Milwaukee hotel.

Going into the final series of the 1974 season, New York desperately needed to beat the Brewers if they were going to catch the Baltimore Orioles, who had mounted a furious late-season drive in September to overtake the Yankees for first place.

But a wild chain of events sparked by a vicious brawl between Rick Dempsey and Bill Sudakis—Thurman Munson's backups—ended up killing their postseason chances.

Dempsey, a hotheaded 24-year-old who had come to the Yankees from Minnesota a few years earlier in a minor trade, was constantly at odds with Sudakis, a first baseman/DH who was technically the third-string catcher but whose skills behind the plate were considered no match for Dempsey's.

That Sudakis was the inferior receiver was something Munson constantly rode him about, which of course made Sudakis resent Dempsey even more.

Especially after a long team flight and a few too many cocktails.

On September 30, the Yankees were coming off just such a flight and some of them had been passing the time by having more than their share of cocktails, first at the airport bar in Cleveland and then on the plane. Sudakis and Dempsey among them.

By the time their bus from the airport pulled up outside the Pfister, a charming old hotel in downtown Milwaukee dating back to the 1890s, a well-oiled Sudakis had been baiting Dempsey for hours.

Sudakis had already called Dempsey out on the bus with threats of "I'm going to kick your ass," and, in a booze-addled variation on "pistols or swords?" had asked Dempsey whether he preferred his ass-kicking via street fighting or old-fashioned boxing.

The stage was set for what most witnesses recalled as a knock-down, drag-out fight akin to a Hollywood-style Wild West brawl.

As both men walked through the revolving doors of the Pfister lobby, Dempsey, nearly as tall as the 6'1" Sudakis but 50 pounds lighter, turned on the bigger man in a mad-dog frenzy, landing a succession of furious, unanswered punches as several Yankees—Munson and all-star outfielder Bobby Murcer among them—tried in vain to separate the two while horrified hotel guests looked on.

Not only were bodies flying as Dempsey swung at anything that moved, Sudakis or not, lobby furniture went airborne, too. Tables and chairs were overturned, and some accounts have the Pfister's long, antique floor lamps being turned into makeshift javelins.

Order was finally restored when Munson put

Dempsey in a headlock.

While several of the half-dozen or so Yankees who jumped into the melee suffered nothing worse than a few bumps and bruises, the biggest casualty turned out to be Murcer, who effectively ended his season in the Pfister lobby.

And maybe the Yankees' season, too.

Murcer, who led the team that season with 88 RBI despite only hitting ten home runs, would miss the crucial two-game series against the Brewers with a jammed finger and strained shoulder as a result of trying to play peacemaker.

His injuries were felt by the entire team the next night. Ironically, it was his absence in the field instead of at the plate that may have cost the Yankees a shot at the A.L. East title.

New York was holding on to a slim 2-0 lead in the eighth inning thanks to a gritty performance by pitcher Doc Medich, who was going for his 20th win. But with one out and the bases empty, Brewers pinch hitter Bob Hansen lifted a fly ball that soared between Yankee centerfielder Elliott Maddox and Lou Piniella, who usually manned leftfield but had replaced Murcer in right.

Both outfielders raced for the ball...and both watched it drop between them, each thinking the other had called for it. Hansen, meanwhile, scooted to third on a gift triple. The Little League move was immediately followed by a line drive that Maddox, in a misguided attempt to make a shoestring catch, instead let the ball get by him for another gift triple. A sacrifice fly later, and the score was tied 2-2.

The Brewers would go on to win it in the tenth on

a bases-loaded, walk-off single off a tired Medich. The bitter loss handed the A.L East title to Baltimore, its fifth in six years.

It was of little solace to the Yankees that they had fought hard until the bitter end, going a respectable 89-73 in 1974 for a second-place finish behind the mighty Orioles. Everyone felt the game should have been won—most of all Piniella, who refused to ponder the strange set of circumstances that started with some drunken needling among teammates, turned into a violent brawl that benched the regular right fielder, and ended up with an out-of place replacement giving up on a fly ball that gave away the season.

"I could have caught it easy," said a distraught Piniella after the game. "If you can't catch that ball, you don't deserve to be in baseball."

# Chapter Twenty
## Goose Goes over the Cliff

The season after the Yankees pulled together to pull off one of the most amazing comebacks in baseball history, the team went straight over the Cliff.

A handful of players who had been an integral part of the 1978 squad that overtook the Red Sox from 14 games back to steal the pennant, and then won a second straight World Series against the Dodgers, were either gone or going in 1979—a year of transition, turmoil and tragedy that began with a battle of behemoths in a clubhouse bathroom and hit bottom with the death of Yankee captain Thurman Munson.

The biggest loss was the trade to the Texas Rangers of reliever Sparky Lyle, the charismatic southpaw who had gone, in the infamous words of quipster Graig Nettles, from Cy Young in 1977 to "sayonara" once flame-throwing free agent Goose Gossage became the closer.

The '79 season also featured future Hall of Famer Catfish Hunter and 20-game-winner Ed Figueroa winning six games between them all year as they both suffered sore arms; the surprising midseason trade of catalyst Mickey Rivers to the Rangers, and the firing

82

of manager Bob Lemon not even halfway into the season for Billy Martin, the man he had replaced the previous year.

And, of course, the ultimate shocker: the 32-year-old Munson's fatal plane crash in early August that sapped the life out of the organization as a whole.

But the Yankees' quest for a three-peat in 1979 was essentially doomed after the first two weeks of the season, when some good-natured clubhouse ribbing sparked an all-out brawl between Gossage and reserve catcher/designated hitter Cliff Johnson that sidelined the closer for most of the year.

According to Gossage, the mid-April fight had been instigated by—who else?— Reggie Jackson, who was goading Johnson about how well he had fared batting against The Goose when both were in the National League.

"I said, '[Johnson] couldn't hit what he couldn't see," Gossage recalled in an interview years later. "I didn't mean it as a knock against Cliff; I was just talking about my velocity."

But the damage had been done—Goose had ruffled Johnson's feathers, and there was only one way to resolve this perceived insult to his manhood.

Gossage said an angry Johnson followed him into the bathroom and challenged him to a fight. "I'm standing at the urinal, [and] I realize Cliff is over my shoulder, telling me, 'You think you can back that shit up?' I'm thinking, 'This guy's not kidding,' " said Gossage.

The pitcher claims Johnson took the first swing, hitting him with an open hand to the neck; Gossage countered with a punch that sent Johnson sprawling into a stall.

But after several teammates rushed in to break up the fight between two of the biggest men on the team—Johnson was a 6', 4' 225-pounder, while the 6'3" Gossage weighed in at 215—a still-miffed Johnson was out for blood.

"Guys are rushing in, breaking it up, so I stopped hitting him," Gossage recalled. "But I'm shouting at Cliff, 'You worthless piece of shit!' So now he tackles me in the shower. I lose my balance and as I'm falling back into the wall, I tear my thumb. Completely tore it up. That was it for my season."

Not quite, though Gossage would be on the shelf for nearly half the season with a torn ligament in his right thumb and would get only 18 saves. The shower room scuffle placed Johnson's head on the trading block, and he was dealt two months later to the Cleveland Indians for pitcher Don Hood.

In an ironic twist, the fight occurred during a weekend series against the Rangers and overshadowed the return to New York of Sparky Lyle—who was promoting his new book, *The Bronx Zoo*, a now-classic tell-all about the dysfunctional Yankee teams of the late 1970s.

Despite the requisite turbulence that year, the Yankees would somehow manage to win 89 games, but it was only good enough for fourth place.

"What a horseshit season that was," Gossage said. "The fight, losing Thurman; worst time of my career. It was terrible. And it all started over nothing."

# Chapter Twenty-One
**Nettles vs. Reggie**

Given Reggie Jackson's outsized ego and natural gift for alienating opponents and teammates alike, it's no surprise he would eventually get into a physical altercation with one of his Yankee brethren.

And considering Graig Nettles was never one to back away from a fight (see: Lee, Bill; or Brett, George), it's also hardly surprising the third-baseman would be the first one to take a swing at Reggie.

What is a shocker is that it took so long for it to happen.

It was near the end of Jackson's fifth and last season with the team when Nettles finally did what scores of Reggie's teammates past and present had no doubt been dying to do: Punch the mouth that had been roaring for years.

The Yankees had just swept Martin's upstart Oakland A's in the 1981 American League Championship Series, and the team, their family and friends were gathered in an Oakland restaurant for the obligatory celebration.

Nettles, the quick-witted, slick-fielding slugger who manned third base for the turbulent Yankee teams of the late 1970s, had reason to celebrate more than most that night. He had carried the team in the three-game rout of Martin's scrappy, "Billy Ball" A's, winning ALCS MVP honors for a hitting performance worthy of Mr. October—Jackson—himself.

In Game 1, Nettles' three-run double in the first inning was all the Yankees needed in a 3-1 win at home. He was the star again in Game 2's 13-3 beatdown of their former manager's team. Nettles ignited a seven-run outburst in the fourth—an inning in which he singled twice—then capped the win with a three-run homer in the seventh.

In a nailbiter Game 3 in Oakland started by AL Rookie of the Year Dave Righetti, the Yankees held a slim 1-0 lead in the ninth when Nettles' bases-loaded drive was misplayed into another three-run double, clinching a 4-0 victory and the pennant.

Nettles' line for the series was 1 HR, 2 doubles, 9 RBI (three ribbies in each game) and a .500 average.

Jackson, meanwhile, was a non-factor in the series. He went hitless in the first game, then left Game 2 after one at-bat when he hurt himself running the bases. He wouldn't return to the lineup until the fourth game of the World Series against the L.A. Dodgers.

But Reg- *gie*, not one to be overshadowed in October, certainly made his presence known at the clinching party when he found himself on the wrong end of a one-sided, one-punch tussle with Nettles.

The official story at the time, at least according to Nettles, was that some people had sat down at the table where his wife and kids were sitting, and they "were a little rude to her and [we] didn't know who the people were," he said.

The people turned out to be Jackson's friends, and when the right fielder came over to ask Nettles what the problem was, "we had a little argument, a little shoving and that was about it," said Nettles, adding that "it was no big deal and I was looking for him later to apologize and he was gone already."

Jackson, for his part, called the incident "a bizarre and unfortunate thing. It was a weird circumstance, a crazy happening and very unfortunate."

Yankees owner George Steinbrenner, who helped break up the altercation, downplayed it as well, calling it "a shoving match as far as I'm concerned. It was an in-house thing, and I don't regard it as very important."

Of course, that's not what eyewitnesses said—or what the New York papers reported. As far as intra-team fights go, it was huge, especially coming on the cusp of the World Series. Not only did it involve the vaunted New York Yankees, it was a future Hall of Famer vs. one of the top third-basemen of his time; together they'd retire with a combined total of nearly 1,000 home runs and 3,000 RBI.

The tale of the tape had Jackson, 35, 6 feet tall and a muscle-bound 190 pounds, taking on the 36-year-old Nettles, also 6 feet tall and weighing in at 180, in what may have started as a heated, alcohol-fueled shoving match but was described by one witness as "a big brawl" involving several star players—Ron Guidry, Goose Gossage and Willie Randolph among them—plus Steinbrenner and Yankees' security personnel all trying to separate the lefty sluggers.

(In a 2009 interview, then-catcher Rick Cerone gleefully described Steinbrenner rolling around on the floor with a bunch of other tangled bodies.)

Peace was finally restored, but it didn't end there. Minutes later, Nettles and Jackson stepped into another room, more words were exchanged and Jackson slapped a bottle of beer out of Nettles' hand.

That's when Nettles, who had gotten six hits in a dozen at-bats in the ALCS, unofficially added one more to the total—he popped Reggie in the mouth, putting the big guy down.

Years later, Nettles would admit the truth in an interview, proudly stating it was indeed a one-punch fight in which Jackson "didn't have time" to get his licks in.

It wasn't the first time Jackson had mixed it up with a teammate. As a member of the A's in 1974—a championship team just as dysfunctional as those late-'70s/early '80s Yankees—he and outfielder Billy North got into a clubhouse tiff that was broken up by teammates. The two were at it again minutes later as the bad blood between the men—Jackson had accused North of dogging it weeks earlier—finally boiled over.

While there were several versions of what happened in that Oakland restaurant, there was no denying Nettles and Jackson made up on the flight home from Oakland the next day.

The 1981 season, though, wouldn't end on a happy note, with the Jackson-Nettles melee soon to be a forgotten footnote to an otherwise bizarro World Series loss to the Dodgers.

In what would turn out to be the final Yankee postseason for Mr. October—and the team's last playoff appearance for another 14 years— the Yanks would cough up a two-games-to-none lead and lose the Series in six amid the embarrassments of manager

Bob Lemon's mystifying moves, a 1-for-22 performance from $20 million man Dave "Mr. May" Winfield and a public apology to New York fans for the loss from Steinbrenner, whose claims of fighting two phantom L.A. fans in an elevator only added to the circus atmosphere.

## Chapter Twenty-Two
**Don't Mess with The Boss**

Call it the Phantom Menace: Two young guys from Los Angeles who, on the night of Oct. 25, 1981, made the mistake of insulting George Steinbrenner's Yankees during an elevator ride with George at the Hyatt Wilshire Hotel.

The Yankees had just dropped three straight games to the Dodgers in Los Angeles, falling behind 3-2 in the World Series, and these fans were gloating, calling Steinbrenner's players chokers and disparaging New York fans.

Steinbrenner first responded with an obscenity and when that wasn't enough, he went fist city. By the time the elevator had descended to the lobby from the seventh floor, where these men got on, Steinbrenner had wiped them out with three fierce punches.

"There are two guys in this town looking for their teeth and two guys who will probably sue me," he said at a hastily arranged press conference.

The only thing missing from Steinbrenner's account of the encounter was "Float like a butterfly, sting like a bee."

Well, actually, one other thing was missing: any sizable group of people who believed him.

Yes, his left hand was in a cast, and yes, witnesses confirmed he had ridden the elevator, entering from the penthouse on the 11th floor.

Notably absent, however, was any evidence of the two young fellows who, by Steinbrenner's account, were perps turned victims.

They have never come forward, nor have any collaborating witnesses.

Steinbrenner's story also had some holes through which Sherlock Holmes could have driven a horse and carriage.

Once the elevator leaves the seventh floor, where Steinbrenner said his opponents got on, its estimated travel time to the lobby is 14 seconds. That's not a lot of time for an argument, an obscenity and a multi-punch fight involving three people.

Three days later, a freelance writer named Philip Greenlee told Randy Harvey of the *Los Angeles Times* that he was in the elevator with Steinbrenner and one other kid, who was indeed obnoxious.

"They started calling each other names," said Greenlee. "When the elevator reached the lobby, Steinbrenner said, 'Nobody makes fun of my Yankees' and banged his fist on the elevator wall. He said, 'Ouch,' and glared at the kid. That was it."

That would account for the cast, if not the story. On that score, there was speculation Steinbrenner was looking to motivate his collapsing team.

A better idea, some Yankee fans thought, was for Steinbrenner and manager Bob Lemon not to decide before Game 6 that they would pull starting pitcher Tommy John early and finish the night with relievers.

Lemon did just that. The Dodgers won the game, 9-2, and thus took the Series.

The Elevator Fight story lived on, however, as a cherished footnote in both Yankee and George Steinbrenner lore.

Why? Well, because during the 37 years Steinbrenner was principal owner of the Yankees, he repeatedly behaved like a knuckleball in a hurricane.

He'd barely owned the team a year when he was convicted on 14 counts of illegal contributions to the Richard M. Nixon election campaign.

He hired and fired Billy Martin as manager five times. They were reportedly in negotiations for round six when Martin died in a car crash on Christmas Day 1989.

Before the 1981 season, Steinbrenner ordered 50,000 yearbooks destroyed because he didn't like his picture.

After his star outfielder Dave Winfield went 1-for-22 in that 1981 World Series, Steinbrenner called him "Mr. May."

Later he paid gambler Howie Spira $40,000 to dig up some dirt that would give Steinbrenner grounds to void Winfield's contract. That gambit earned him a lifetime ban later reduced to 30 months.

After his prize Japanese free agent pitcher Hideki Irabu failed to live up to what Steinbrenner paid him, Steinbrenner called him a "fat, pussy toad."

When the Indians upset the Yankees in the 1997 playoffs, Steinbrenner went on an off-season rampage that included threatening to cut everyone's dental plan.

He should have just threatened to knock out their teeth.

## Chapter Twenty-Three
**Fisk vs. the Yankees**

Up until the day Pedro Martinez face-planted 72-year-old Don Zimmer into the Fenway grass in the 2003 ALCS, the Red Sox player that Yankee fans most loved to hate was undoubtedly Carlton Fisk.

High praise, considering you can fill a 40-man roster with all the annoying players who have worn a Boston uniform throughout the teams' long and bitter rivalry.

The Yankeefication of such Sox stars as Wade Boggs, Roger Clemens and Johnny Damon would take most of the sting out of fans' vitriol for at least those players, especially after they helped the Bombers win a few rings.

And it's hard to actually hate the always-entertaining Manny Ramirez for being a clueless man-child, or David Ortiz for styling after putting one over the fence. It was Reggie, after all, who practically patented post-dinger showboating.

But for any Yankee fan who was around in the '70s, Fisk was the poster boy for Red Sox revulsion. There was plenty of reason to loathe him, boo him and—if you were stealthy enough to sneak into the box seats near the plate at the Stadium late in a game against Boston—jeer him up close for having one ball.

We're not talking pitcher's count here.

Early in his career, the Sox catcher suffered one of the most gruesome injuries ever seen on a ballfield, one that even the most ardent Yankee fan wouldn't wish on a Red Sox player. Unless it was Pedro Martinez.

Squatting behind the plate in a spring training game on March 17, 1974—St. Patrick's Day—Fisk took a foul tip right to his clovers. The ball smashed his protective cup, ruptured a testicle and caused him to pass out from what had to be the same sort of unimaginable, indescribable pain that comes from watching a light-hitting Yankee shortstop snatch a pennant away with a pop-fly homer.

The fact that Fisk would recover from such a frightening—and yes, embarrassing—injury and go on to catch another 20 years in a Hall of Fame career is certainly admirable. But it doesn't take away from the fact that he was a loathsome figure to loyal Yankee fans.

It wasn't just his matinee idol looks or that silly "stay fair" dance he performed on his Game 6 walk-off homer in the 1975 World Series.

The No. 1 reason for hating Fisk was this: Thurman Munson did.

So did Munson's teammates. And therefore, so did every Yankee fan.

As the two best up-and-coming young catchers in the American League of the early '70s, Fisk and Munson were constantly being compared to each other. Both were Rookie of the Year winners, both were hardnosed catchers who had emerged as team leaders, both were good hitters at a position where defense was traditionally more important than offense.

But with a little more pop in his bat and with the Sox being a little bit better than the Yanks in those years, Fisk usually got a little bit better press, much to Munson's chagrin.

And so on a hot afternoon at Fenway Park, with New York and Boston in the midst of a four-team, late-summer pennant race, the modern-day rivalry that has defined the Yankees-Red Sox universe for the past four decades was created.

And it happened with a big bang: A collision of stars at home plate.

On August 1, 1973, the AL East was still up for grabs with just one-third of the season to go. New York was in first place, one game ahead of Baltimore and two in front of Detroit; Boston was in fourth, just 3.5 games back.

In the top of the ninth inning of a 2-2 game, Munson, who had doubled to lead off the inning, was dancing off third with one out and another runner on first. With Fisk calling the signals, shortstop Gene Michael stepped into the box and squared to bunt—a daring suicide squeeze that failed miserably.

Despite his thick, squatty build, Munson was a surprisingly good base runner. He was halfway down the line when he realized he was hung out to dry— Michael had missed the pitch. With Fisk waiting at the plate, ball firmly in hand, Munson did the only thing he could: try to separate the catcher from the ball.

The fact that it was his chief rival, standing there ready to be run over, put a bit more pep in Munson's step. Head down and shoulders square, Munson barreled into the larger man, a sudden impact of flesh, bone and catcher's equipment that sent both players sprawling. Munson ended up on top of Fisk, with the Red Sox catcher trying to kick his Yankee rival off of him so that he could prevent the other Yankee runner from advancing any further.

It would have been just another bang-bang, game-saving play except Munson took exception to Fisk's kicking him, Fisk didn't appreciate Michael not getting out of his way as Munson came thundering down the line, and Michael didn't like Fisk digging his elbow into his ribs to knock him aside.

What followed was a classic benches-clearing brawl after Munson slugged Fisk. Michael jumped the catcher from behind as Munson was being held back by a couple of Red Sox players. Michael, a tall, skinny shortstop nicknamed Stick, clawed and scratched and tried to get a few punches in before Fisk put him in a headlock.

The Red Sox weren't as miffed at Munson as they were at Michael, deriding the "cheap shot" he took at their catcher. But mostly they were mad that Michael got to stay in the game while the umpires tossed Munson and Fisk.

"[Michael] jumped me from behind and grabbed me by the face and started scratching and punching," said Fisk in the clubhouse, sporting a few nasty scratches on his chiseled mug. "That skinny fucker was the guy they should have thrown out."

Bill Lee, a flaky Red Sox southpaw not-so-affectionately known as the Spaceman, took one look at Fisk's face and summed up the Yankees' fighting skills as a bunch of hookers swinging their purses.

It was a great line, one the Yankees would file away for later.

The fight—and the game, which New York would lose, 3-2, in the bottom of the ninth—proved to be a turning point in what would quickly become a sorry season. The loss knocked the team back into a first-place tie with the Orioles, who would go on to win the division. The Yankees would go 20-33 the rest of the year and end up in fourth place, 17 games out. The Red Sox would creep past them, finishing second.

Even worse—especially for new owner George Steinbrenner—the crosstown rival Mets would stagger into the World Series that year with a paltry 82-79 record, not much better than the Yankees' 80-82. It would also be the end of Ralph Houk's second stint as manager.

Sitting in the cramped visitor's clubhouse at Fenway after the game, Munson had no idea how badly the season would turn out. The future Yankee captain was living in the moment, trying hard not to show how much he had enjoyed taking it to his bitter rival despite the tough loss.

"We said a few things and I hit him," said Munson about Fisk, a small smile visible under his walrus mustache. "Is he scratched up? What a fucking shame."

## Chapter Twenty-Four
### The Rematch: Spaceman Falls to Earth

It took nearly three years for the bad blood between the Yankees and the Red Sox to boil over again. And when it did, it made the Fisk/Munson melee of 1973 look like, well, a bunch of angry hookers swinging their purses.

On May 20, 1976, the Bombers took on the Bosox in the first of a four-game series in the Bronx that had an October feel despite it being so early in the season. The Yankees—playing at the recently renovated Stadium for the first time in two seasons and looking like a playoff contender thanks to several new additions and a fiery Billy Martin at the helm—were in first place with a commanding six-game lead over fourth-place Boston, the defending American League champions.

The game was turning into a gem, with new Yankee righty Ed Figueroa holding a slim 1-0 edge over New York nemesis Bill "The Spaceman" Lee, the out-there lefty who was nearly as big a lightning rod as catcher Carlton Fisk when it came to the long-simmering Yankees-Red Sox rivalry of the '70s.

Lee, of course, had angered the Bombers after the

1973 brawl between the teams by uttering the famous quip about the Yankees fighting like they had purses. As the game headed into the bottom of the sixth inning, the Spaceman was about to be brought down to earth.

Just like three years earlier, a Yankee barreling into Fisk during a play at the plate would spark a vicious, bench-clearing brouhaha. With outfielder Lou Piniella on second and third baseman Graig Nettles on first, the next batter scorched a line-drive single to Dwight Evans, the Red Sox right fielder with a cannon arm.

To no one's surprise, the throw got to Fisk well ahead of the lumbering Sweet Lou, who, like Munson years before, put his head down and attempted to separate the hated Fisk from the ball.

And just like three years earlier, Fisk, sensing Piniella was out for blood, set himself for a collision, then put a hard tag on the runner and came up swinging. Which of course kicked off the long-awaited rematch.

As a pile of twisted bodies tussled around the plate, pushing and punching and wrestling—and as Mickey Rivers, the new Yankee centerfielder, was sucker-punching anything in a gray Boston uniform in the back of the head—Lee emerged from the pile with a pained expression, baseball cap askew like an '80s rapper and left arm slung low.

Nettles, apparently still a bit sensitive over Lee's earlier "purse" comment, had body-slammed the pitcher to the turf and separated his throwing shoulder.

As if the injury wasn't bad enough, Lee promptly made it worse.

Order was beginning to be restored, but an angry Lee made the mistake of looking for Nettles in the crowd with one arm out of commission. The pitcher, lifeless left limb at his side, finally found the hotheaded infielder and began jawing at him.

Even the most amateur lip reader could easily pick up what Lee called Nettles, and it wasn't "glasshole."

Nettles' reply was a lightning-quick, right-left combination that put Lee on his wallet—and incited both teams to start swinging again. Whereupon Rivers made huge points with the by-now rabid fans in the stands by jumping into the fray one more time and resumed punching Boston players in the back, including Lee.

The Red Sox ended up winning the game, but the brawl took a huge toll on the team, which lost a good pitcher coming off three consecutive 17-win seasons. Boston, which had taken the Cincinnati Reds to a Game 7 in a thrilling World Series the year before, staggered to a third-place finish in 1976. They ended up 15.5 games behind the Yankees and wouldn't get a whiff of the postseason for another decade.

Though the Yankees would get steamrolled by the Big Red Machine in October, the fight helped unify a team that, like the Stadium, had been pretty much overhauled over the winter. It also proved ballplayers have long memories.

"[Lee] just tried to sneak around the pile and he came at me, getting in my face," said Nettles after the game. "I wanted to make sure he wasn't hit with any purse."

# Chapter Twenty-Five
**Hanging Chad**

When today's Yankee fans think back fondly to the great Bomber teams of the late-'90s dynasty, it's easy to overlook Chad Curtis.

Despite being the regular leftfielder on the 1998 juggernaut that won a then-record 114 regular season games and went 11-2 in the postseason, the contributions from Curtis—solid defense, middling production (10 HR, 56 RBI, .243), good speed (21 SB)—are overshadowed by the achievements that year by such marquee Yankees as Jeter, O'Neill, Martinez and Williams, and grinders like third baseman Scott Brosius.

Curtis, a journeyman who broke in with the California Angels in 1992, won two World Series rings and had his crowning achievement with New York, the fourth of six teams he'd play for in a 10-year career. As a platoon player in 1999, he started Game 3 of the World Series against the Atlanta Braves and led the Yankees back from a 5-1 hole with a pair of home runs, the last coming in the 10th inning for a walk-off win that put the Yanks up 3-0 in their eventual Series sweep.

His accomplishments that brisk October night also clued in the rest of America on what diehard Yankees fans—and Curtis' past and present teammates—already knew. The short, crew-cutted Curtis was a self-righteous, proselytizing Bible-thumper who wasn't afraid to get in anyone's face if they didn't live up to his old-school baseball code. Or his Christian ethics.

The requisite post-game interview on national television after his big home run never happened—Curtis snubbed NBC's Jim Gray for the harsh way the sideline reporter had treated Pete Rose during a recent interview with the disgraced star.

It was the second high-profile run-in that year for Curtis—the first of which likely resulting in his being traded away after the 1999 season. During a game in August against the Seattle Mariners at Safeco Field, Curtis went after the wrong guy during a benches-clearing brawl.

His teammate and Yankee icon, Derek Jeter.

A fight between New York catcher Joe Girardi and Seattle pitcher Frankie Rodriguez in the ninth inning, precipitated by an exchange of beanballs, resulted in the usual pushing and shoving after Rodriguez landed a flurry of punches on the future Yankees skipper.

Order was eventually restored but the hostilities didn't end there. It seems that Jeter had never entered the fray. He spent it on the fringes of the scrum, yukking it up with the Mariners shortstop—his then-pal, Alex Rodriguez—while the rest of the Yankees were upholding pinstripe pride and honor.

For Curtis, whose clubhouse routine included leading the players' Sunday morning chapel service, seeing Jeter fraternizing with the enemy instead of sticking up for his teammates was tantamount to worshiping Satan. In full view of the cameras, Curtis confronted the young star on the steps of the Yankee dugout, a brief but heated exchange that was broken up by a Yankee coach.

Curtis was probably right about Jeter's behavior—once can only imagine how Billy Martin would have slammed his shortstop, star or not. But Curtis compounded the issue later that night by approaching Jeter again in the clubhouse in front of reporters

"There's a little difference of opinion there," Curtis said later.

"We can have a difference of opinion," Jeter retorted. "Everyone in a bench-clearing brawl isn't fighting. You have guys trying to break things up, guys talking, guys trying to control the situation. That's how it goes sometimes."

No matter who was right, Curtis ended up the loser. He was traded to the Texas Rangers for a pair of minor leaguers in the off-season, weeks after his World Series heroics. Though the Yankee front office denied it, Curtis—not the most popular guy in the clubhouse to begin with—felt his squabble with Jeter was what got him banished from the Bronx after two championship seasons.

"If the people that are making the decisions decide there's a conflict there that's going to rub a little bit, and one of us has to go, are you kidding me?" Curtis would later say. "What kind of idiot is going to send [Jeter] out of there? That is absolutely a no-brainer."

# Chapter Twenty-Six
## Lowering the Boom on Boomer

David Wells pitched for the Yankees in the wrong era.

Cocky, colorful and a tad too corpulent for a modern-day conditioned athlete, the loudmouthed lefty would have no doubt ran with the Babe—his idol—on Ruth's nightly sojourns to the speakeasies and bawdy houses of the Roaring Twenties; been part of the hard-drinking clique led by the unholy trinity of Mickey, Whitey and Billy in the Eisenhower '50s; or fit right in with the squabbling, larger-than-life Bronx Zoo teams of the late '70s.

"If I could come back as anybody, it would be Babe Ruth," Wells said upon signing with the Yankees. "Especially the way he carried himself off the field."

Unfortunately for Wells, aka "Boomer," his two, two-year stays with the Yankees coincided with the buttoned-up, all-business image of the late '90s/early '00s dynasty personified by Derek Jeter and skipper Joe Torre, the latter reluctantly putting up with the antics of the talented but troublemaking southpaw as long as he was winning.

Which Wells did often, especially in the

postseason. He went 34-14 in his first stint with the Yanks in 1997-98, highlighted by a perfect game against the Minnesota Twins at the Stadium in May 1998.

He'd return to the team for the 2002 and 2003 seasons, again going 34-14 over a two-year span. His postseason record for the Yankees, which included a World Series championship in 1998, was a sparkling 8-2.

But among the highlights were a slew of shenanigans, silliness and outright instances of stupidity that helped run Boomer, for all his wins and clutch performances, out of town. Twice.

The ink was barely dry on the three-year, $13.5 million free-agent contract Wells signed with the Yankees before the 1997 season when the portly pitcher and a pal got into a late-night street fight with two other men in Wells' hometown of San Diego.

The Yankees, who were well aware of the 33-year-old Wells' reputation as, to put it politely, a free spirit, couldn't have been pleased. It was bad enough that their big, new free-agent acquisition, weeks before he even donned the pinstripes, was facing felony assault charges after one of the men he fought had to be hospitalized.

But Wells' bad first impression got worse: He had also broken a bone in his pitching hand during the scuffle, rendering him useless for a good chunk of spring training.

There would be other less serious, but no-less-annoying hijinks during his Yankee career. Like the time Wells wore a cap that had belonged to the Babe in the first inning of a game in 1997. The hat, which Wells bought for $35,000, earned the pitcher a hefty fine from Torre, who apparently wasn't nearly as amused as everyone else seemed to be.

Or like the time Wells glowered from the mound at some of his fielders, including Jeter, for muffing a pop fly that fell between them. Showing up his teammates on the field, a huge no-no for a team-first player like Jeter, resulted in the shortstop giving the pitcher a verbal dressing-down in the dugout.

But none of that comes close to what would prove to be Wells' most embarrassing incident in pinstripes—which occurred, naturally, in the wee hours and after the pitcher was seemingly in his cups and out of uniform.

In September 2002, the 39-year-old Wells was eating with a friend in an Upper East Side diner when he exchanged some words with fans seated at a nearby table. But things would soon turn ugly. One of the men, a 27-year-old, 5'7" bartender named Rocco Graziosa—nine inches shorter and about 80 pounds lighter than Wells—took exception to something the pitcher said and then proceeded to punch the hefty lefty, knocking him down and knocking out two of his teeth.

A small guy lowering the boom on big, bad Boomer was bad enough, but Wells suffered through a further embarrassment when the tape of his 911 call to the cops was soon made public.

The pitcher was heard slurring his words as he called his assailant a "fucking Italian, little squatty-body motherfucker," the capper to a bad night on the town that would have made even the Babe cringe.

# Chapter Twenty-Seven
## Clemens Goes Batty

Roger Clemens and Mike Piazza didn't much like each other before Piazza came to bat against Clemens in the first inning of Game 2 of the 2000 World Series.

Four pitches later, they really really didn't like each other.

They had also ensured that their considerable baseball legacies would always include the footnote that they were involved in one of the most puzzling moments in the history of the game.

Yes, weirder than Jimmy Piersall running the bases backwards when he hit his 100th home run.

The backstory between Clemens and Piazza was about three months old on Oct. 22, 2000.

In July, when the Mets and Yankees played a regular-season game, Clemens had hit Piazza in the head with a fastball, which as dealt by Clemens moved about 98 miles an hour.

Piazza was uninjured and unimpressed. This wasn't a brushback pitch that sailed, Piazza would later write in his autobiography. Clemens had pinpoint control, so if the ball hit his head, Clemens had aimed at his head. In the rematch, at Shea Stadium, the Yankees hadn't scored in the top of the first.

Clemens struck out the first two Mets in the bottom of the inning and the first three pitches to Piazza were uneventful. A ball, two strikes.

The fourth pitch broke in on his hands and he swung, looking mostly as if he wanted to fend it off.

The ball dribbled foul down the first base side. The bat shattered into three pieces.

Piazza held onto the grip. A small middle piece flipped off to the side.

The barrel shimmied out toward the mound, ending up in front of it and slightly to Clemens' left.

Piazza started to run slowly up the first-base line, still holding the bat handle, just in case hurricane-force winds erupted and blew the ball fair.

Clemens hesitated a second, then took a couple of quick steps, picked up the barrel and threw it toward the first base line, in front of where Piazza was running.

By then and by chance, Piazza was looking toward Clemens, so he slowed down and let the bat pass in front of him.

He looked perplexed, then turned and yelled at Clemens, "What the fuck's your problem?"

Clemens looked away, perhaps distracted by the sound of both benches emptying and converging on the mound.

Piazza's teammates got between him and Clemens. He made no serious move to engage, later admitting in his autobiography that he was well aware the much larger Clemens might "kick my ass" on national television.

He also said he should have rushed him anyway, because it was just something a man should do in that situation.

Clemens pretty much ignored Piazza, keeping his game face, which was not smiley in the happiest of times.

Piazza eventually returned to the plate. On the next pitch he grounded out to second base.

Clemens was hardly rattled by the bat-toss moment. He pitched eight innings and allowed just two hits, leaving with a 6-0 lead that became a 6-5 victory when the Mets scored five runs off the Yankees bullpen in the ninth.

In any case, the post-game questions for Clemens started with the bat barrel toss.

He said he threw it because he first thought it was the ball.

Of course he did. He's a pitcher. He doesn't handle a real ball very often, so how could he be expected to know the difference?

The fact he threw it toward Piazza, rather than following the more standard baseball protocol of throwing to first, suggested he also might have momentarily assumed they were playing dodgeball.

However murky Clemens's motivation, at least one subsequent fact is indisputable. Thirteen years later, a Texas auction house sold the barrel, which Yankee strength coach Jeff Mangold said he retrieved from the trash, for $47,800.

The whole peculiar moment by then had also folded into a larger, sadder story.

In the first inning on Oct. 22, 2000, Mike Piazza batting against Roger Clemens looked like a showdown of two surefire future Hall of Famers— Piazza, maybe the best-hitting catcher ever, Clemens, a dominant pitcher who would end his career with 354 wins and 4,672 strikeouts.

When they became Hall-eligible for the first time, however, both fell short. Piazza got 57.8% of the votes his first year, below the 75% needed for election (though he would be elected in 2016). Clemens got 37.6%.

The reason was no mystery. Both had been linked to the use of performance-enhancing drugs. Both denied it, which apparently wasn't enough, at least in their first years of eligibility.

In Clemens' case it probably didn't help that he was also widely regarded as a jerk—and the events of Oct. 22, 2000, did little to dispel that particular perception

# Part III
# BLUNDERS

# Chapter Twenty-Eight
## The Cellar Years

Lest anyone suggest Yankees fans have become spoiled, consider that in the first four years the New York Mets were in business, from 1962 to 1965, they finished last as many times as the Yankees finished last in the entire 20th century.

Still, that was little consolation in the fall and winter of 1966, following a season in which the Yankees did finish last, for the first time in 54 years, and the Mets thundered past the Chicago Cubs over in the National League to finish a proud ninth.

Numbers rule baseball with a singular ruthlessness, and no number holds more power than the "W." When a season ends and every other team in the league has more, it has been a bad season.

And yes, even the Yankees have had seasons like that.

Take 1908.

Fifty-one W's. One hundred and three L's. The Highlanders finished 16 games behind the American League's next worst team, Washington.

No one saw that one coming, either. Two years earlier, the Yankees had won 90 games, just three fewer than the pennant-winning White Sox. Al Orth led the league with 27 wins and Jack Chesbro added 24.

To look at it another way, in 1906 the team's two top pitchers won as many games as the whole team won in 1908. Chesbro's record in 1908 was 14-20. Orth went 2-13.

Things picked up the next couple of years, then imploded again in 1912, when the team only won 50 games and lost 102.

Ironically, 1912 is more often remembered by Yankees fans for several other reasons.

That was the team's last year in Hilltop Park, which would be demolished two years later and is now part of Columbia Presbyterian Hospital. The Greater New Yorks played in the Polo Grounds for the next decade until Babe Ruth finally built them a house of their own in 1923.

More important, 1912 was the first year for the pinstripe uniform with the interlocking NY on the chest.

The new uniform was dropped after that season, amid a few whispers that the new uniform must be bad luck. It returned for good in 1916.

Some say 1912 was also the last year the team was called the Highlanders, though considerable evidence suggests "Yankees" had already been coming into common usage.

Whatever mojo was at work, New York has not lost 100 games in a season since then and the team would not finish last again for 54 years.

The 1966 season wasn't as disastrous as 1908 or 1912, though once again it marked a precipitous decline. The Yankees had made the World Series just two years earlier, in 1964, and they still had Mickey Mantle.

But Mickey's knees were crumbling, and they took the team with him. The Yankees' batting average in 1966 was .235 and even the hits they did get came at the wrong times. They went 15-38 in one-run games.

A last-week surge, with four wins in the last five games, brought the team's final record to 70-89, still half a game behind the Red Sox.

This was arguably the lowest point in what most Yankees fans consider an extended low point: the team's ownership by CBS.

Over the eight years CBS owned the team, 1965-1972, it went 636-646, which would have been fine if the Yankees were the Indians or the Senators or the Seattle Pilots. Which they were not.

Once George Steinbrenner bought the team in 1973, the picture brightened. By 1976 they were back in the World Series.

After a loss to the Dodgers in the 1981 Series, though, another 15-year drought cycle set in, and this one bottomed out with another last-place finish in 1990.

The team's record was 67-95. They were shut out 15 times, blown out 28 times and went 0-12 against Oakland.

The most amazing statistic of 1990 was that Steinbrenner only fired one manager, Bucky Dent, when the team started 18-31. Stump Merrill finished the season and was even allowed to manage the next season, though he was fired after that.

For the record, the Mets have now finished last 13 times.

# Chapter Twenty-Nine
## Jack Chesbro's Wild Pitch

The first 454 1/3 innings of Jack Chesbro's 1904 season went better than the last 1/3.

Still, looking back 110 years, it hardly seems fair that when a fellow throws 454 2/3 innings and wins 41 games in a single season, with 48 complete games and a 1.82 ERA, he has to spend the rest of his life being asked about one bad pitch he threw while chasing that last out.

Welcome to Jack Chesbro's world.

With two games remaining in the 1904 season, the future Yankees—then known as the Greater New Yorks or the Highlanders—trailed Boston by a game and a half for the American League pennant.

But the faithful had hope, because New York was playing Boston in both those games—a doubleheader at Highlanders Park.

Some 30,000 fans jammed the field, lining both baselines and surrounding the outfield.

"Probably no such interest ever was taken in a baseball event in this city as was manifested in the doubleheader of yesterday," the *Times* reported the following day.

And that wasn't even the best omen.

The first game starter would be Chesbro, whose 41 wins would stand for the rest of the century as the most by a pitcher in a single season.

As Chesbro's innings total would suggest, Highlanders manager Clark Griffith wasn't a strict pitch count kind of guy.

Griffith also wasn't an "every five days" kind of guy. The October 10 start would be Chesbro's eighth in 15 days, and frankly, there were some signs his arm might be wearing down.

In his previous outing, two days earlier, Boston had knocked him out en route to a 13-2 victory.

Still, you want your best pitcher in your biggest game and on October 10 that was still "Happy Jack."

Relying on the spitball, then a legal pitch, Chesbro shut out the Bostons for six innings. New York, meanwhile, scored twice in the fifth to take a 2-0 lead.

In the seventh, however, Boston got a runner on first and New York second baseman Jimmy Williams fumbled a potential double-play grounder, leaving runners at first and second.

A sacrifice bunt moved them up and when another grounder was hit to Williams, his low throw to the plate skipped past catcher Red Kleinow and allowed both runners to score, tying the game.

Come the top of the ninth, score still 2-2, Boston catcher Lou Kriger reached third with two out and Freddy Parent at bat.

With the count at 2-2, Chesbro tried to blow Parent away with a spitter. Unfortunately, the pitch was what blew away. It rifled past Kleinow, allowing Kriger to score what would stand as the winning run. Boston 3, New York 2.

Game, set and pennant to Boston.

The New Yorks would have to wait 17 years for their first championship—though, if it's any consolation, they wouldn't have gone to the World Series even if they won the pennant in 1904. The petulant John McGraw, manager of the National League champion Giants, said the American League wasn't a real major league and declared his Giants to be champions of the world without no stinking Series.

As for that pitch, Chesbro later said it wasn't uncatchable, that even though spitters were notorious for their unpredictable path, Kleinow could have at least blocked it.

Not everyone agreed. New York shortstop Kid Elberfeld said it sailed so high Kleinow would have needed stilts to catch it. Contemporary newspaper accounts also had it soaring over the rookie catcher's head.

Its precise trajectory will remain an eternal mystery, 30,000 witnesses notwithstanding.

Not surprisingly, Chesbro never had another year like 1904. A fellow can throw 454 2/3 innings only so often. But he won 19 and 24 games the next two years and finished his career with 193 wins.

For the rest of his life, inside and outside baseball, he fielded questions about that pitch.

After he died in 1931, his widow Mabel spent another eight years trying to convince Major League Baseball to go back into the official box score and change the ruling from a wild pitch to a passed ball.

She didn't succeed.

But in 1946 he did get elected to the Hall of Fame. For the 41 wins, not the one wild pitch.

## Chapter Thirty
### Carl Mays and the Ribbon of Darkness

They say Carl Mays was the most disliked player in all of baseball during his career, which is no minor superlative considering he was a contemporary of Ty Cobb.

It's a little like being the biggest publicity hound in a room that also includes Donald Trump.

A century after his big league career began, though, the fact Mays struck his peers as a jerk has faded into a footnote.

What baseball remembers is that on Aug. 16, 1920, a sidearm fastball from Carl Mays struck Cleveland Indians shortstop Ray Chapman in the head and killed him.

It remains the only fatality from a pitched ball in Major League history.

August 16 was a dark, overcast day at the Polo Grounds, where the Yankees played home games before Yankee Stadium was finally built.

The Indians, who would go on to win the World Series that season, had a 4-0 lead going into the fifth inning.

Chapman, batting leadoff, was a righty. So was

Mays, whose low submarine delivery seemed to come from halfway to third base.

Chapman liked to crowd the plate. Mays liked to brush off batters who crowded the plate.

The pitch came inside and high and while Mays later said Chapman ducked into it, almost everyone else on the field said Chapman never moved. Probably never even saw it.

But everyone heard it. Babe Ruth, playing right field, said he heard a crack. Mays thought the ball had hit Chapman's bat. As it rolled back to the mound, Mays picked it up and threw to first.

Decades before batting helmets, the ball had hit Chapman in the temple, fracturing his skull.

He was helped off the field and taken to the hospital. As pressure built, doctors operated, too late. He died at 4:30 the next morning.

Mays said he was sorry and promptly blamed everyone but himself. His assertion that Chapman ducked into the pitch now sounded like, "It was his own fault." Nor did Mays gain much sympathy when he blamed umpire Tommy Connolly for not discarding a "scuffed" baseball, since Mays liked to scuff the ball himself.

While Mays insisted he never threw at anyone, including Chapman, he had had a headhunter reputation since his breakout year of 1917 with the Red Sox, when he led the league with 14 hit batsmen.

After Chapman's death, three teams petitioned the American League to ban Mays from baseball. Players talked of boycotting games in which he pitched.

This didn't bother Mays, who was known to publicly berate his own teammates and clearly cared little about his personal popularity.

The immediate tension dissipated after Indians manager Tris Speaker issued a statement saying the team did not hold Mays responsible—an exoneration Mays himself was happy to adopt and maintain until he died 51 years later at the age of 79.

Far from being troubled, Mays had his career season the following year, going 27-9 to lead the Yankees to their first-ever American League pennant.

In all, Mays would rack up five 20-win seasons and finish his career in 1929 with a 207-126 record and a 2.92 ERA.

He may not have had a Hall of Fame personality, but those are Hall of Fame numbers, which begs the question of why Mays is not in the Hall and by all accounts has never come close to election.

The standard explanation is Chapman's death, that it just casts too dark a shadow on a man who essentially blamed the victim.

But some baseball historians point to another possible reason, one tied much more closely to Mays's sour disposition and the suspicion he was only in it for himself.

After his spectacular 1921 season, Mays started the first game of the World Series—the first Yankee to throw a World Series pitch.

He shut the Giants out that day, scattering five hits.

He started game 4 and had another shutout with a 1-0 lead through seven innings. Two more innings and the Yankees would have a healthy 3-1 lead in the best-of-nine Series.

But the Giants' Irish Meusel led off the eighth with a triple, then scored on a single to tie it up. Frank Snyder laid down a bunt and Mays fell trying to field it, leaving two on.

A sacrifice that Mays did field moved the runners up and they both scored on a double. The Giants added a run in the ninth and won the game, 4-2.

Mays came back in Game 7, giving up six hits and one earned run, but losing 2-1.

For the Series, which the Yankees lost 5-3, Mays pitched 26 innings with a 1.73 ERA. Those are ace numbers, though his record was only 1-2.

Bad luck?

Fred Lieb, one of the most influential and connected sportswriters of the era, said maybe not.

Lieb said he fell into conversation with Yankees co-owner "Cap" Huston, whose tongue was loosened by a few drinks, and that Huston told him Mays had thrown those last two games.

The allegations made it to Kenesaw Mountain Landis, the commissioner who a year earlier had thrown eight Black Sox out of baseball forever.

This time Landis said he found no compelling evidence of malfeasance. Mays was cleared.

Lieb stuck to his story, which he said was later collaborated by Yankees manager Miller Huggins.

Huggins told writers that Mays was one of only two players he had ever managed—the other was Joe Bush—that he wouldn't help in a time of need. If he found Mays in the gutter, Huggins said, he'd kick him.

Lieb, perhaps not incidentally, had an influential voice in the Hall of Fame—where he was ultimately enshrined himself.

Whatever the real story, no one has ever had to figure out what to say on a Carl Mays Hall of Fame inscription.

# Chapter Thirty-One
**Babe's Mad Dash**

The World Series didn't get its first Game Seven walk-off HR until 1960, when Bill Mazeroski—well, if you either love or hate the Yankees, you know that story.

Thirty-four years earlier, however, the 1926 Series ended with something even rarer: a Game 7 walk-off CS.

Ironically, the guy who was CS that day was more famous for hitting HRs.

Babe Ruth was nailed with a strike from St. Louis Cardinals catcher Bob O'Farrell to second baseman Rogers Hornsby as Ruth tried to steal second base with two out in the bottom of the ninth inning and the Yankees trailing 3-2.

The question today is the same one that was asked 87 years ago. What in the name of God was he thinking?

Two out, two grade-A sluggers coming to bat with Bob Meusel and Lou Gehrig.

Why risk everything?

Well, Ruth's defenders say he had his reasons, and they tend to buy 'em.

First, they point out, advancing from first to

second base in that situation is hardly incidental. It means the runner, who will be in motion with the crack of the bat, doesn't need an extra-base hit to score. A single will do it.

That's the thinking by which Mike Davis stole second base before Kirk Gibson's home run against at the A's in 1988. More painfully for Yankee fans, it was the impetus behind the Red Sox sending in pinch-runner Dave Roberts to steal second base in the same situation in the ninth inning of Game 4 of the 2004 American League Championship Series.

Roberts then did score on a single, which triggered the Yanks' 2004 collapse, another painful story chronicled elsewhere in appropriately excruciating detail.

So back to Babe. He wasn't a great baserunner and he was too big to have great speed. But he was regarded as a smart baserunner, and in this case he tried a delayed steal, hoping Hornsby and O'Farrell would be surprised enough not to execute a perfect throw and tag.

They were surprised. But they executed a perfect throw and tag anyway.

In a larger poetic sense, Ruth's dash provided a final exclamation mark for one of baseball's most dramatic games.

This was the game in which, according to legend, Grover Cleveland "Pete" Alexander of the Cardinals lurched to the pitcher's mound in the seventh inning with a hangover and a problem. The Yankees had runners at the corners with two out and Tony Lazzeri at bat.

Alexander ultimately struck Lazzeri out,

preserving that 3-2 Cardinals lead, but only after Lazzeri had sent a long drive foul into the left field seats.

Alexander, who had gone nine innings to win Game 6 the day before, then retired the side in the eighth and got both Earl Combs and Mark Koenig to ground out to third to start the ninth.

Ruth was up next. He had already hit four home runs in the Series, which may explain why he had also walked ten times. No one wanted to give him anything he could hit, and even through the haze of his hangover, Alexander knew that was sound policy.

He tried nibbling at the corners, ultimately missing with a slow curve on a 3-2 pitch to give Babe walk No. 11.

Meusel and Gehrig on the stat sheet were a couple of solid bets to bring Babe around—Meusel a .300 hitter with power, Gehrig just finishing a strong sophomore year and leading the team in hitting in the Series.

But Meusel had been slumping, going just 5 for 21 in the Series, and the odds of his driving an extra-base hit off Alexander were not great on a wet day with a soggy ball.

That's probably what in the name of God Ruth was thinking as he took off for second.

Seconds later, it didn't matter. Umpire Bill Dineen's right thumb went up and like President Calvin Coolidge's fiscal regulatory policies, Babe's bet didn't come in.

## Chapter Thirty-Two
**Bevens Blows It**

Cookie Lavagetto's last hit in the Major Leagues came on Bill Bevens's last pitch in the Major Leagues.

Just a 35-year-old journeyman third baseman playing out the string and a 30-year-old pitcher who'd lost the magic, but didn't leave the party before one last toast that no one was likely to forget.

It was a drama that no one could possibly have predicted on Oct. 3, 1947, as the Yankees and Dodgers prepared for Game 4 of the World Series at Ebbets Field.

The Dodgers, trailing the Series 2-1, were sending Harry Taylor to the mound. He was ticketed as the Dodgers's next big pitching star, with just one problem. He had torn a tendon in his arm. Since those were the days of manly men when they didn't mollycoddle pitchers, manager Burt Shotton sent him to the mound anyway.

Taylor was relieved after four batters, none of whom he retired. And oh, by the way, his career was effectively over.

Bevens, coming off a 7-13 regular season, had no trouble retiring batters. Inning after inning, he mowed the Brooklyns down.

Well, he mowed down the ones he didn't walk. He issued 10 walks for the game and two of them, in the fifth, led to a Brooklyn run.

Still, Bevens led 2-1 going into the bottom of the ninth, at which point Brooklyn was still looking for its first hit.

At this point, nine years before Don Larsen, there had never been a no-hitter in postseason play.

Dodgers Catcher Bruce Edwards opened the ninth with a drive that went almost to the wall. Almost. One out.

Carl Furillo walked. Naturally.

Spider Jorgenson fouled out to first. Two out. One more and Bevens would have the first no-hitter in World Series history.

Al Gionfriddo ran for Furillo as Pete Reiser pinch-hit for Hugh Casey.

On a 2-1 pitch, Gionfriddo stole second, putting him in scoring position. With the count now 3-1, Yankee manager Bucky Harris ordered Bevens to walk Reiser, ignoring the long-standing baseball custom of never putting the potential winning run on base.

Shotton sent Eddie Miksis in to run for Reiser, who had a bum ankle, and he sent Lavagetto up to bat for leadoff man Eddie Stanky.

Lavagetto swung at the first pitch and missed. He swung at the second pitch, just a fraction late, and connected.

But let's back up a few beats and let Red Barber, who was then the Dodgers' announcer and would later move to the Yankees, narrate the story:

"Gionfriddo walks off second ... Miksis off first ... They're both ready to go on anything ... Two men out, last of the ninth ... the pitch ... swung on, there's a drive hit out toward the right field corner. Henrich is going back. He can't get it! It's off the wall for a base hit! Here comes the tying run, and here comes the winning run! ... Friends, they're killin' Lavagetto... his own teammates... they're beatin' him to pieces and it's taking a police escort to get Lavagetto away from the Dodgers! Well, I'll be a suck-egg mule!"

That's one way to put it.

# Chapter Thirty-Three
**Casey and Elston**

George Weiss, the general manager who in the 1950s
ruled the Yankees the way Robert Moses ruled New
York city planning, didn't see integration of the Major
Leagues as an opportunity.

It was more like a nuisance.

Weiss, who of course was not alone in holding
that view, had an official statement when he was asked
why, six or seven years after Jackie Robinson started
playing for Brooklyn, the Yankees still were all-white.

It went like this: "The Yankees will bring up a
Negro as soon as one that fits the high Yankee
Standards is found."

As it happens, we have some evidence concerning
the intensity of that search.

On June 11, 1950, the Yankees sent scout Bill
McCorry to the Polo Grounds to check out a
Birmingham Barons outfielder named Willie Mays.

After the report from McCorry, a long-time
intimate of Weiss, the Yankees decided not to pursue
Mays.

The Giants signed him nine days later, on June
20, the same day Kansas City Monarchs owner Tom

Baird wrote the Yankees a letter saying they might be interested in "a hell of a player" he just signed, "a 19-year-old shortstop named Ernest Banks."

Nah, the Yankees weren't interested.

In 1951, the Yankees did sign Victor Pellot, professional name Vic Power, to a minor league contract.

In 1952, he batted .331 for the triple-A Kansas City Blues and led the American Association in doubles and triples. In 1953, he led the same league with a .349 batting average.

In neither 1953 nor 1954 did the Yankees invite him to spring training—a decision that played awkwardly in the press, which noted that it was now seven years since Robinson broke in with Brooklyn.

Power was soon traded to the Philadelphia Athletics. Dan Burley, a writer who had been lobbying forever to get baseball off the segregation dime, wrote that the Yankees still wanted a black player who knew his place.

Power, it was whispered inside the organization, wasn't the "right" black player.

Too flamboyant, too outspoken. Too colorful, so to speak.

Instead, the Yankees broke their color line with Elston Howard, who was signed in 1950 and made his Yankee debut on April 14, 1955.

Howard always said he was treated well by the Yankees and his teammates. It wasn't their fault, he said, that he had to stay with a local black family in St. Petersburg during spring training because Florida segregation laws wouldn't let him stay with the rest of the team.

There was also the matter of manager Casey Stengel, with whom the concept of "treated well" needs to be placed in the context of the times.

Stengel is widely reported to have spoken some close variation on the line, "They finally get me a n----- and I get the only one that can't run."

Whether that's apocryphal is anyone's guess. It's true Howard was slow on his feet, though to most listeners that wasn't the important half of the sentence.

Most serious baseball fans understood, then and now, that Casey wasn't just the lovable old "crazy like a fox" character who embedded himself so deeply in the baseball lore of the 1950s.

Casey had a sharp tongue, a mean streak and a vocabulary straight out of the place he grew up, early 20th-century Kansas City.

He had no hesitation in nicknaming Howard "Eightball." Writer Steve Jacobsen, in his book on the integration of baseball, says Stengel also referred to Howard as "my j--."

"He was particularly insulting to blacks," Roy Campanella's son Roy Jr. told writer David Cataneo. "He was a racist who used [the n-word] as if he thought it were appropriate."

On the flip side of that coin, others say Stengel simply came from a time when those words were part of the general conversation.

"Casey was a racist only in the casual, unthinking way most of his generation of Americans were," Stengel biographer Robert Creamer told Cataneo. "Racial and ethnic slurs were characteristic of his era."

Once Howard's value to the Yankees was established, Stengel praised his skills and named him to multiple all-star teams. Arlene Howard noted that she and Elston also developed a personal friendship with Stengel and his wife Edna.

Still, the Yankees weren't in any hurry to plunge more deeply into racial waters once Howard's playing career ended.

Howard made no secret of his desire to be a manager, and under boss George Steinbrenner, he was hired as a coach. But while Steinbrenner was giving everyone this side of Richard Nixon a chance to manage the Yankees in the mid-'70s, he never called Howard's name.

Asked about this, Steinbrenner said he had bigger plans for Howard.

Whatever those plans were, they died along with him in 1980.

As for Vic Power, he reflected some years later on his Yankee experience. Keep reading.

132

## Chapter Thirty-Four
### Vic Power: The Yankee Who Wasn't

Vic Power said that late in his baseball career, which took him to the A's, Indians, Twins, Phillies and Angels, he developed a stock response to writers who asked why he was never called up to the team that first signed him, the Yankees.

"I'd answer," Power told writer Danny Peary, "that they were waiting to see if I could turn white. But I couldn't do it."

Thems could have been fighting words. Power, in his 60s when he talked to Peary, showed little sign of anger.

How could a kid from Puerto Rico whose mother fed six children by sewing dresses complain about getting paid to play a game that left him the time and opportunity to develop and indulge a passion for good food, art and music all over America?

His only real complaint with the Yankees, he said, was that after he hit .294 for Triple-A Syracuse in 1951 and .331 for Triple-A Kansas City in 1952, he wasn't even invited to spring training the following years.

"They'd said, 'Vic Power didn't prove to us he

can hit a Major League pitcher.' Well, how could I when I'd never seen a Major League pitcher?"

After he hit .349 back at Kansas City in 1953, leading the American Association, it would have been hard not to give him a look in Florida in spring 1954.

Yankee General Manager George Weiss made that point moot in December 1953 by trading Power to the Philadelphia Athletics.

The A's had also never had a black player. The main immediate difference was that the A's were so bad they could have used the Purple People Eater.

Power hit only .255 his first year in the Bigs, when the A's moved him from first base to centerfield and wouldn't let him use his favored 36-ounce bat, saying it was too heavy.

The following year, with a new manager who returned him to first base and gave him back the big bat, he hit .319, finishing second to Al Kaline in the American League batting race.

This performance ensured that the question of why the Yankees dumped him didn't get a rest.

He was a showboat, some said. On the field, he favored one-handed catches with a grand flourish. Off the field, he cruised the town in a big old white Cadillac convertible whose front passenger seat was known to include white women.

He also believed in fighting back, although he insisted he only got aggressive when someone else made the first move, like pitchers who threw at him.

"When Bill Skowron or Bill Renna homered, the pitchers would throw at my head," he said. "I had to protect myself."

Power said he was "friendly" with Elston Howard,

who became the first black Yankee once Power had been traded.

"But I thought he was too much of a yes-man," said Power, a complaint he also had with other early black players like Junior Gilliam.

Howard, said Power, "wasn't my competition because he wasn't a star. If the Yankees wanted to bring up a black player, they couldn't justify picking him as long as I was in the organization."

His experiences in the Yankee organization, as Power remembered them, were frustrating in small ways that ran through the bloodstream of both baseball and America in those not so distant days.

His minor league Yankee teammates "were friendly on the field," he said, "but I wondered why they'd drive past me when I was walking two miles to the colored section. I thought they were afraid of breaking a municipal law.

"We'd stop at restaurants and I'd have to stay on the bus, which I didn't mind, but not once did a teammate or the manager offer to bring me something to eat."

Once he came up to the Majors and played against the Yankees, he said, a few players didn't seem to like him, including Hank Bauer and Jim Coates. He said Mickey Mantle didn't like him either, a feeling that was mutual and mostly professional.

"I told him I didn't like that he made all that money," said Power, "and wouldn't run to first on a grounder."

But Yogi Berra, he liked. Phil Rizzuto, he liked. Billy Martin, "the first time I played against him he came over and shook my hand. We got along beautifully."

135

And Casey Stengel, the manager with the old-school ethnic vocabulary?

"I loved Casey," said Power. "He always told me he wished I had been a Yankee."

Power remembered a game against the Yankees in the late '50s when Stengel brought in Ryne Duran, the proverbial hard-throwing right-hander. Duran also had notoriously bad eyesight and wore dark glasses, which added to the trepidation hitters already felt about facing his fastball.

"He threw a fastball behind my back," said Power. "I got up and walked over the Yankee bench, where everyone was laughing. I told Casey, 'Listen, old man, if he hits me, I'm not going to fight him. I'm going to fight you.' Casey just kept laughing."

Looking back, Power told Peary, what he regretted about his Yankee non-career were those two seasons when he burned up Triple-A. He was 24, 25. They were prime years. He could have been hitting Major League pitchers, scooping up Major League throws. He could have added a couple more All-Star games to the four in which he played and a couple more Gold Gloves to the seven he ended up collecting.

But he wasn't angry, he said. Better to laugh.

He apparently got that from Casey.

## Chapter Thirty-Five
### Gil McDougald and the Line Drives

Gil McDougald had one of those batting stances that you shouldn't try at home, kids.

He spread his legs far apart and cocked his bat—well, that's the thing. He didn't really cock his bat. He held it in back of him, but almost parallel to the ground, somewhere between shoulder and waist level.

It sounds like a good strategy for Wiffle ball.

McDougald stood that way for ten seasons in the Major Leagues, winning the American League rookie of the year award in 1951 and batting .276 over his career.

Not bad for a middle infielder.

"Maybe McDougald does hold the bat cockeyed," Casey Stengel remarked during spring training of his rookie year. "But there ain't nothing wrong with the way he swings it."

For the record, McDougald had developed that stance back in college. Made it easier for him to hit the curve ball, he said.

It also made him into a line drive hitter. With less torque than the guys who started their swing somewhere around the third base dugout, he tended not to swing for the fences.

Not that he needed to. His 1950s Yankee teams had plenty of other guys for that. McDougald ended up with 112 of the quietest career home runs in baseball history.

Fellow Yankees from those years remember McDougald as a straight arrow on a team that liked to have a good time. No Copa brawls for Gil. He was a family man with seven children. He was also a devout Catholic who spoke frequently about the value of prayer.

Even if prayer couldn't redirect a couple of tragic line drives.

The second of those line drives remains one of baseball's great tragedies—the ruined career of Cleveland Indians pitcher Herb Score.

By 1957, his third year in the Majors, Score was the Next Big Pitching Thing, the guy who was going to pick up where the legendary Bob Feller left off.

Score had been American League rookie of the year in 1955, going 16-10 with a league-leading 245 strikeouts. The next year, he upped it to 20-9 with 263 strikeouts.

On the night of May 7, 1957, he took the mound against the Yankees. In the bottom of the first, one out, nobody on, Score threw a 2-2 fastball to McDougald. It was just the pitch for which McDougald was looking and he drove it back up the middle, smashing into Score's face just above his right eye.

The ball caromed to third baseman Al Smith, who threw to first. McDougald ran toward the mound.

Score was rushed to a hospital, where he was diagnosed with multiple bone fractures that threatened the sight in his eye.

Later that night McDougald went to the hospital, where he was told Score could not have visitors.

McDougald told writers that if Score lost his sight, "I'm going to quit the game." He also said he was praying. He remained shaken after a letter from Score and his family, saying they held no grudge and it was just an accident of baseball.

Score would regain his sight, though he did not pitch again in 1957. The next season, trying to come back, he tore a tendon in his arm. He struggled through five more seasons, winning a total of 19 games and never reaching .500. He retired at 30.

Years later, McDougald told the *Los Angeles Times*, "I guess I didn't pray hard enough. I feel that I jeopardized a good living for him. He had a lot of years ahead of him, good years. If there was anything I could do, I'd do it. But there's nothing. All I can do is pray."

Less chronicled is the line drive that had a similarly severe impact on McDougald's own life.

During batting practice on Tuesday, Aug. 2, 1955, before a night game with Cleveland at Yankee Stadium, McDougald was struck on the left side of the head by a line drive from teammate Bob Cerv.

The team doctor and an eye specialist examined him in the clubhouse and said it was just a concussion. He was taken to Lenox Hospital, observed and discharged.

By Saturday he was back in the lineup, going 1 for 4 against Billy Hoeft of the Tigers. On Sunday he played both ends of a doubleheader.

The doctors who approved his return had missed something, though: a small skull fracture and corresponding damage to the inner ear.

McDougald didn't notice it himself for another two decades.

But by the mid-1970s, when he was coaching the Fordham baseball team, he found it increasingly hard to hear his players. The problem became so acute that in 1976, he resigned.

His hearing continued to deteriorate until, by the late 1980s, he could hear virtually nothing. He gave up his businesses, team reunions and even family dinners, according to a July 1994 Ira Berkow column in the *New York Times*.

A doctor who read the column contacted McDougald and recommended a cochlear implant, which restored enough hearing to give him back his life.

It was a happy ending to a career with several curious footnotes.

McDougald was the runner who was doubled off first when Sandy Amoros flagged down Yogi Berra's slicing fly ball in Game 7 of the 1955 World Series, the play that saved the only Series Brooklyn ever won.

McDougald's last appearance in a Yankee uniform, or any uniform, was Game 7 of the 1960 World Series. He entered in the ninth as a defensive replacement at third base, where he got to turn his head and watch Bill Mazeroski's game-winning home run disappear over the left field wall.

In between, a couple of seemingly random line drives became the straight arrow's defining moments.

# Chapter Thirty-Six
**Tony Kubek's Rocky Day**

According to University of Pittsburgh geological experts, the sedimentary rock under the city of Pittsburgh runs to a depth of more than 16,000 feet.

It's a particularly durable gift to the city from the late Paleozoic Era.

Little did the Paleozoics know that some 300 million years later, a tiny random chip of that rock would decide the 1960 World Series.

True, most fans think the seventh game of the 1960 World Series, played in Pittsburgh's Forbes Field, was decided by Bill Mazeroski's walk-off home run off Ralph Terry in the bottom of the ninth, giving the Pirates a 10-9 win in one of the most exciting baseball games ever played.

Were it not for that tiny chip of rock embedded in the notoriously hard and rocky Forbes Field infield, however, Terry might never have been in the game and Mazeroski may never have come to bat. And incidentally, Mazeroski probably never would have made it to the Hall of Fame, though that's another story.

In the game itself, the Yankees overcame an early

4-0 Pirates lead by scoring one in the fifth, four in the sixth and two in the eighth, making it 7-4 New York.

Pinch-hitter Gino Cimoli singled to right to lead off the Pirates' eighth. But Bobby Shantz then got Bill Virdon to rifle a ground ball right at Yankee shortstop Tony Kubek, who alongside Bobby Richardson formed a machine-like double-play combination from 1959 to 1965.

Kubek glided over to field the ball, except the pebble had other ideas. The ball skipped up and smashed into Kubek's throat. He dropped faster than the 1964 Phillies and the ball rolled away for what was officially scored a single

Arthur Daley, writing the next day, said Virdon's grounder was "spitefully steered by Dame Fortune," who on this day was disguised as the pebble.

What-if's are a fool's errand in baseball, but had Kubek and Richardson doubled up the slow-footed Cimoli and Virdon, Shantz would have had two out and none on.

Instead, it was the other way around.

A Dick Groat single scored Cimoli, bringing in reliever Jim Coates. He got two outs before Roberto Clemente topped a slow roller to the right of the mound.

First baseman Moose Skowron scarfed it up and would have tossed to Coates at first for the third out except Coates wasn't there. He had started for the ball instead. Virdon scored to make it 7-6.

Arguably five outs into the inning, the Pirates sent catcher Hal Smith to the plate. The former Yankee prospect wasn't a big threat. He'd hit only three home runs all year.

Oops, make it four, so just about the time Kubek was arriving at the hospital, the Pirates led, 9-7.

The Yankees tied it in the top of the ninth.

Then Mazeroski came up and that was that.

Kubek was released from the hospital the next day, after a few scary hours when he couldn't speak.

When he did regain his speech, it wasn't to talk about that ground ball. Years later, when he was a baseball broadcaster, his partner Bob Costas started to bring the subject up and Kubek touched him on the thigh to let him know not to.

What was there to say, really? He was 300 million years too late.

# Chapter Thirty-Seven
## Red Barber Gets Shorn

And then there was the day they shot the messenger.

Except this messenger wasn't a minimum-wage kid trying to thread a bicycle down a Manhattan cross street.

This messenger was Walter Lanier Barber, universally known as "Red" and just as universally known for being one of the most revered baseball announcers of all time.

Back when he broadcast Dodgers games in the 1940s, he was known for folksy Southern phrases like "sitting in the catbird seat" and "tearing up the pea patch."

But on Thursday, Sept. 22, 1966, announcing for the Yankees, he got serious.

The Yankees, stumbling to a last-place finish, were playing an afternoon makeup game against the equally played-out Chicago White Sox.

Paid attendance was 413, fewer people than were waiting on a lot of subway platforms.

The game was televised and Yankee management had ordered the camera crews not to follow foul balls into the stands, lest all those empty seats be revealed to even a modest viewing audience.

Barber was not so protective.

"I don't know what the paid attendance is today," he told the TV audience, "but whatever it is, it is the smallest crowd in the history of Yankee Stadium, and this crowd is the story, not the game."

Barber couldn't get the cameras to pan the stands, either. But he had made his point, and at least one person was listening.

By sheer coincidence, this was the first game for Mike Burke as president and chairman of the Yankees. He was also a vice president at CBS, which had just bought the team.

The day before, Burke had told the media that while he planned to improve the team on the field, he saw no reason to change the broadcast team, which also included Phil Rizzuto, Joe Garagiola and Jerry Coleman.

Then Burke heard Barber analyze the attendance.

On Monday, Sept. 26, Burke invited Barber to breakfast and told him his $50,000 contract would not be renewed.

Barber told reporters he left the meeting after "a cup and a half of coffee ... If they don't need me, I don't want to be with the Yankees."

Neither Barber nor Burke cited the New York 413 as the reason for Barber's dismissal. Burke said that despite his own vote of confidence to Barber a few days earlier, the CBS board had made the termination decision "two weeks ago."

That embarrassing stumble foreshadowed Burke's and CBS's whole ownership tenure, which ended when some guy named Steinbrenner bought the team in 1973.

Barber put a stoic face on it. Here, after all, was a guy whose career had begun back on April 17, 1934, in Cincinnati, when he did play-by-play for the first Major League game he ever attended.

"My best years are ahead of me," he said after his meeting with Burke. "I want to broadcast in baseball on a job where I am welcome."

Didn't happen. After his final Yankees contest on Sept. 29, also against the White Sox, he never called another baseball game.

# Chapter Thirty-Eight
## The Cheapest Win Ever

With all the games the Yankees won in the 20th century, it was inevitable some would stir and exhilarate fans for many decades.

Babe Ruth's called shot. Don Larsen's perfect game. Reggie Jackson's three. Bucky Dent. It's a long list.

There was also, arguably, a worst win, and it came on Sept. 30, 1971, in Washington, D.C.

For both teams this was the final game of long mediocre seasons. The only Yankee incentive, if anyone much cared, was that a win would enable the team to finish above .500, at 82-80.

The Senators didn't even have that. They came into the game at 63-95 and that wasn't even the saddest part.

After this game, owner Bob Short was moving the team to Texas, marking the second time in a decade that an owner had decided Washington D.C. couldn't support baseball—or in the case of both Washington teams, losing baseball.

The Senators' biggest name was their manager, Ted Williams, who for most of the season had spent more time thinking about fishing than how to win games with a lousy team.

An official count of 14,460 fans showed up for the game, which wasn't a bad turnout for a wake, and as the game went on, their mood turned ugly.

Security personnel seemed disinterested or absent, letting some of the rowdier fans act out.

Management did manage to remove a couple of homemade banners with messages like "Short Sh---," but a handful of fans started running onto the field and more than a handful hurled random objects.

Meanwhile, the teams did play a baseball game. Dick Bosman started for the Senators and the Yankees quickly took a 4-0 lead.

But in the sixth inning, with the Yankees up 5-1, the Senators created one last memory for Washington.

Frank Howard started the inning with a home run into the left field seats.

The crowd rose to its feet and wouldn't stop cheering, paying tribute to the only player who'd given the team any spark the last two years, the only one they'd really miss.

He came out and waved his cap.

Mike Kekich, the Yankee starter, was coy later about the pitch Howard hit.

Specifically, he didn't deny he might have laid it in there, figuring a Howard homer would be the little gift he could throw to a city about to lose its team.

In any case, the Senators were inspired enough to score three more runs and tie it up at 5.

They then added another couple and were leading 7-5 going into the ninth.

By this late hour, the remaining fans were feeling

a visceral sense of the end. A crowd that had mostly been frustrated was turning angry. More objects were landing on the field, more fans jumping the barriers.

Announcements over the public address system pleaded with fans to remain orderly.

Meanwhile, Washington reliever Joe Grzenda got pinch-hitter Felipe Alou and leadoff man Bobby Murcer to hit comebackers.

Horace Clarke was heading toward the plate when a small wave of fans rolled onto the field. The Senators' bullpen pitchers, tired of watching for projectiles and not wanting to get trapped in something ugly, left the pen in left-center field and ran across the field toward the dugout.

That seemed to shatter any less shred of restraint. Clarke never got his at-bat as fans poured onto the field, oblivious to further warnings over the PA system that if the field wasn't cleared, the game would be forfeited.

At this point like, yeah, the fans cared.

Moments later the PA announcer said fine, it's a forfeit.

The teams retreated to the locker rooms, while the fans did some spirited if largely superficial trashing.

Among the items strewn about and tossed onto the field were paperbacks of Williams' autobiography. The team had put them out in the walkways, along with other leftover promotional items it figured it might as well give away rather than throw out.

Good move. It would be 33 years before Washington got another baseball team.

For purposes of baseball history, the Yankees officially won the game and finished the season 82-80, 21 games behind the Baltimore Orioles.

It was one of only five forfeits in baseball since 1955, joining, among others, the infamous Disco Demolition night at Comiskey Park in Chicago in 1979.

This one was cheaper, smaller and sadder than that one.

Grzenda, talking to reporters after the game, said he just wished the fans could have held off for another five minutes.

He could have closed this one out, he said. He'd never had any trouble with Horace Clarke.

## Chapter Thirty-Nine
### The Hot Dog Gets a Candy Bar

At first there were just a few, square little orange discs sailing out of the stands and landing on the freshly manicured opening-day grass of the most storied baseball field in the world.

Then there were more, and still more, until they filled the air like great showers of rain.

Or, in this case, great showers of Reggie! Bars.

With Reggie Jackson, nothing was ever simple, routine, easy or quiet. Not even a candy bar giveaway.

When it came to Reggie! Bars, honestly, they were not a good candy bar. But as projectiles, fans clearly felt they had real potential.

Reggie signed with the Yankees after the 1976 season, a moment of pure serendipity.

The Yankees, after being swept by the Reds in the 1976 World Series, figured they needed one more bat.

Reggie, for his part, had finished his glory days in Oakland and been marking a little time in Baltimore while he yearned to get to the big city and all that big media attention.

"If I played in New York," Reggie had once cracked, "they'd name a candy bar after me."

151

The 1977 season had rough stretches, but sure enough, the Yankees got to the Series again and this time they breezed past the Dodgers, 4-2.

In the sixth game, Reggie hit three home runs in three consecutive at-bats, showing precisely the flair for which George Steinbrenner committed a then-eye-popping $3 million over five years.

It's not bragging if you can do it, and Reggie's big-stage profile was not lost on Standard Brands Confectionary, which decided Reggie was right. This man deserved his own candy bar.

Unlike Reggie himself, the Reggie! Bar was more safe than flamboyant. It was primarily peanuts with a corn syrup sweetener, coated with chocolate and packaged in a square orange wrapper with a picture of Reggie swinging the bat. It sold for a quarter.

The Yankees agreed to introduce it in a big way, giving a free one to everyone who attended the 1978 home opener on April 13.

The Yankees didn't open the season at home, though. They opened on the road and lurched to a 1-4 start, which already had Steinbrenner muttering out loud.

But 44,667 fans showed up on Opening Day at the Stadium and in the bottom of the first, Mickey Rivers and Willie Randolph got on base.

That brought Reggie up against Chicago White Sox pitcher Wilbur Wood, a knuckleballer.

Jackson took two balls, then swung at a knuckler—his first swing at the Stadium since he sent his third and last home run into the bleachers against the Dodgers the previous October.

A moment later, this ball too disappeared over the fence in deep right-center.

The fans, looking for an appropriate response, started throwing Reggie! Bars.

Hundreds, thousands of Reggie! Bars sailed onto the grass down the right and left field lines. For five minutes the fans stood on their feet and chanted "Reggie!"

White Sox manager Bob Lemon later said someone could have been hurt. He also acknowledged the lighter side of the barrage.

"People starving all over the world," he said, "and 30 billion calories are laying on the field."

Reggie shrugged. "I appreciated it," he said. "It was a nice gesture."

The Yankees won another World Series in 1978. The Reggie! Bar never caught on outside New York and was discontinued in 1980.

# Chapter Forty
## The One That Got Away, 1981

Despite all the Abbott and Costello routines the Yankees and principal owner George Steinbrenner staged in the 1981 World Series—"Mr. May," the public apology, ridiculous pitching moves, the list goes on—the Yankees still would almost certainly have won the Series if they hadn't suffered maybe their most inexplicable postseason loss ever in Game 3.

It had been a weird year already, a season split in half by a midsummer strike. Both the Yankees and Dodgers, who were meeting in the World Series, had played mediocre ball for the last ten weeks before waking up to win their league playoffs.

In the Series, the Yankees kept it in gear and pounded the Dodgers early. A couple of dominant starting pitchers go a long way in a short Series, and the Yankees had Ron Guidry and Tommy John.

In Game 1, Guidry allowed four hits and one run in seven innings, leaving with a 5-1 lead. Ron Davis gave up two runs in the eight, but Goose Gossage closed out the 5-3 win.

In Game 2, John gave up just three hits in seven innings. Gossage closed again, 3-0.

The Yankees now only needed to beat Fernando Valenzuela in Game 3.

This was the year of Fernandomania, when the Dodgers rookie had become the bright glow in baseball's darkened sky, one of the primary reasons fans stayed around through and after the strike.

But the shining star was already showing signs of becoming a shooting star.

Once hitters had seen him a few times, as often happens with rookies, he was no longer untouchable.

In Game 3 of the Series, he couldn't have been more touchable if they had played slow-pitch softball.

The first Yankee batter, Willie Randolph, worked a 10-pitch walk, and Valenzuela said after the game that wasn't the worst of it.

His money pitch was a screwball, which looked tantalizing to hitters right up until it tailed off low and away, and or low and in, or some other place where it was almost impossible to hit.

Pitching to Randolph, he said, he realized the screwball wasn't working. The tease wasn't there. He wasn't swinging.

Valenzuela got out of the inning on a double-play grounder, and the Dodgers gave him some help in the bottom of the first when Ron Cey hit a three-run homer.

But that didn't make the screwball behave.

Valenzuela gave up two runs in the second inning and another two in the third, with Bob Watson and Rick Cerone both hitting home runs.

After Cerone's homer, a two-run shot in the third with Lou Pinella on base, Dodgers manager Tommy LaSorda walked out to the mound.

LaSorda had relievers ready, and when he took that stroll himself, instead of sending pitching coach Ron Perranoski, it almost always meant he was going to ask for the ball.

In a conversation held entirely in Spanish, Valenzuela asked for one more batter. LaSorda said okay, but one more run and that was it.

Aurelio Rodriguez beat out a bunt and went to second on an error. Valenzuela then intentionally walked Milbourne so he could get to Yankee pitcher Dave Righetti, who struck out to end the inning.

Valenzuela survived. But after three innings, he was lucky to have only given up four runs and six hits. He had also thrown 76 pitches.

This was a guy who was ready to be taken.

LaSorda decided, however, that Valenzuela wasn't the guy who needed to come out. Instead he pulled Steve Yeager at the start of the fourth inning and replaced him with Valenzuela's regular catcher, Mike Sciosia. That still didn't fix the screwball, but it settled Valenzuela down.

It also kept in play one of several puzzling Yankees lineup moves.

Reggie Jackson, hero of the 1977 and 1978 series against the Dodgers, had recovered from an injury and was ready to play. But manager Bob Lemon left him out of the lineup.

Lemon said it was so Jackson wouldn't have to face a lefty. Darker whispers said that because Jackson was in the last year of his contract and showed no sign of wanting to come back, Steinbrenner had told Lemon to show Reggie the Yankees could win without him.

Whatever the reason the Dodgers regained the

lead in the bottom of the fifth when they scored twice on a couple of hits, a couple of walks and a double play grounder.

By the end of the seventh, Valenzuela had given up seven hits and seven walks and racked up 136 pitches, more than any manager a few years later would have allowed even a pitching machine to throw.

But he still had the lead when Rodriguez and Larry Milbourne led off the eighth for the Yankees with singles.

With pitcher Rudy May due up, that sent Lemon to his bench.

But he left Jackson sitting on it, instead sending up Bobby Murcer - with instructions to bunt.

That didn't work out so well. Murcer poked at a high inside pitch and the ball popped into foul territory behind the third-base line. Cey made a diving catch and fired to first to double off Milbourne.

Another bullet dodged, Valenzuela closed out the eighth and threw a 1-2-3 ninth. His day's work: nine hits, seven walks, four earned runs, nine runners left on base. He threw 160 pitches.

But he won, and instead of being up 3-0, the Yankees were up 2-1. Three games later they were down 4-2.

Reggie Jackson signed with the Angels on Jan. 22, 1982.

# Chapter Forty-One
## The Day Brett's Head Exploded

One of baseball's most cherished stories, which is probably apocryphal but so what, starts with famed umpire Bill Klem hesitating after a close play on the bases.

The runner, according to the story, snaps, "What am I, safe or out?"

And Klem replies, "You're nothing until I say so."

What makes the story classic is that baseball has a long and proud tradition of giving umpires the last word, even when they are demonstrably dead wrong.

In 2010, to note one particularly poignant example, Detroit pitcher Armando Galarraga lost a perfect game when the first base umpire called the third batter in the ninth inning safe at first.

Every replay showed the batter was out. But the umpire had called him safe, so he will forever be safe.

That may be one reason the Pine Tar Game of July 24, 1983, became so indelibly imprinted in baseball lore—because the umpire, in this case Tim McClelland, was overruled.

This odd breach of baseball protocol cost the

Yankees a game they would have liked to win, because they were fighting a lively pennant race.

In fact, it was a game they thought they had won, by invoking an odd technicality at precisely the right moment.

Specifically, the Yankees were playing the Kansas City Royals at the Stadium and had a 4-3 lead with two out in the top of the ninth.

U.L. Washington was on first base and Goose Gossage was pitching for the Yankees. The batter was George Brett.

Gossage usually won these showdowns. Not this time. Brett, a terrific hitter, sent one over the fence, giving the Royals a 5-4 lead.

As Brett crossed home plate, Yankees manager Billy Martin asked McClelland to examine Brett's bat and determine whether the pine tar, a substance legally applied by many batters to give them a firmer grip, went further up the barrel than baseball rules allow.

The rule set 18 inches as the maximum extension for pine tar. If the coating exceeded 18 inches, the rules stated, the bat was to be removed from the game. If the bat were not removed and the batter got a hit with it, that was to be declared an "illegally batted ball" and the batter ruled out.

McClelland, a rookie, took his time. He held the bat over home plate, which is 17 inches wide.

Finally he walked over to the Royals dugout, pointed to Brett and signaled, "You're out."

Since that was the third out, the game was over and the Yankees had won, 4-3. Brett's reaction measured on the Richter Scale.

He exploded out of the dugout like a rocket-powered grenade and might have vaporized McClelland had Royals manager Dick Howser not intercepted him.

It was a legendary tantrum, one that three decades later remains a favorite on YouTube and that Brett admitted he watches himself at least once a year with his grandchildren, who think it's pretty funny.

The Royals skipped the laughter, though, and filed a protest with American League President Lee MacPhail.

The Yankees weren't too worried. The umpire was always right.

Except here, when he was wrong.

McPhail ruled that Brett had not violated "the spirit of the restriction." The home run stood, the Royals led 5-4 and the game would be resumed with two out in the top of the ninth.

That finally came to pass the afternoon of Aug. 18, an off-day when the Royals were en route to Baltimore.

As a final statement of counterprotest, Martin put pitcher Ron Guidry in centerfield and first baseman Don Mattingly, a lefty, at second base.

It didn't matter. While 1,200 curiosity-seekers watched from the stands, Hal McRae made the final Royals out in the ninth and Dan Quisenberry set down the Yankees 1-2-3.

The Pine Tar Game spawned a country song by C.W. McCall and a lifetime of mostly grumpy comments from Brett, who thought some writers were reducing his Hall of Fame career to a single bizarre incident.

It also spawned some odd jockeying for historical position. Yankees third baseman Graig Nettles claims in his autobiography that he alerted Martin to Brett's pine tar use earlier in the season, and that Martin waited for the right moment to employ the information.

Yankees coach Don Zimmer said he was the one who suggested an appeal to Martin, even as Brett was rounding the bases. Zimmer added that he later regretted it, since it caused such commotion when really, flagging someone for excessive pine tar was like giving a New Yorker a ticket for jaywalking. It wasn't a crime. It was a universal way of life.

Perhaps the most interesting consequence of the Pine Tar Game, though, was not the Yankees losing a game they thought they'd won, or even an umpire being slapped down by his league.

It was the exposure of the Pine Tar rule itself.

As MacPhail pointed out in his decision, the Pine Tar rule had nothing to do with altering equipment to gain an unfair advantage. It was not the batter's equivalent of doctoring the ball.

No, the Pine Tar rule was designed to keep batted balls from being tarnished by pine tar, thus allowing the balls to remain in play for longer.

Yes, that's right. It was designed to save teams a few bucks on new baseballs. Since the average Major League game uses some 120 baseballs, keeping one ball in play for an extra batter or two wouldn't seem to be a big savings.

But MacPhail couldn't say that. Instead, he noted that if a ball is hit out of the park, it wouldn't have stayed in play anyway, so the tarnishing issue was moot and it was not an "illegally batted ball."

And that, Bill Klem, was that.

## Chapter Forty-Two
### Scooter Gets Stepped On

It was Phil Rizzuto's great misfortune as a Yankees broadcast announcer from 1956 to 1996 that much of his tenure overlapped with that of Ralph Kiner's announcing career with the Mets, one borough to the East.

Kiner was such a legend of malaprops and spectacularly butchered simple sentences that he dominated all conversation on befuddled or befuddling New York baseball announcers of the '70s and '80s.

So Rizzuto, as much of a city institution as he became, didn't always get full credit for being a rare piece of announcing work himself.

It was déjà vu all over again for Rizzuto, as his lifelong pal Yogi Berra might have remarked.

As a player, he put in 13 solid years, even won an American League MVP, and yet he was always in the shadow of a Joe DiMaggio or Mickey Mantle.

He gets to the broadcasting booth and it happens again.

He always said he had never planned to be a broadcaster, an assertion no one who listened to him, even those who adored him, would ever doubt.

But on Old-Timers' Day in 1956 the Yankees cut him from the playing roster, deciding he was washed up and they needed to open a spot for Enos Slaughter, who at 39 was a year older than Rizzuto.

Rizzuto fell into the broadcast booth, with no experience, and for the next 40 years he sounded like a guy with no experience.

In a good way.

He knew baseball and he knew the Yankees. He didn't know filters.

But he was thinking about a cannoli joint in Utica, or on his drive home the previous night, the price of getting the Yankees play-by-play was hearing all about it.

Most Yankees fans didn't mind. They didn't mind the night he called a shot to right field a home run and wanted to know why the team was running off the field. Told the right fielder had caught the ball for the third out, Rizzuto said he didn't believe it. He'd already called it a home run. What else did the ball have to do? Go into the stands?

Fans didn't mind that he left games in the seventh inning to beat the traffic over the George Washington Bridge.

They didn't mind that his scorecards were legendarily filled with the notation "WW," meaning "wasn't watching."

They actually enjoyed that he seemingly had no filters.

The night Pope Paul VI died, Rizzuto solemnly said, "That kind of puts a damper on even a Yankee win."

He mused one time that when he went to New Guinea, he expected "to see a lot of Italians."

He declared that "if Don Mattingly doesn't win the American League MVP, nothing is kosher in China."

When the camera panned to a good-looking woman in the stands, Rizzuto said it reminded him of the old song, "A Pretty Girl Is Like a Memory."

Nor did any of this bother him. It got him the nice house, the gig doing "Money Store" commercials, arguably kept him on the radar until the Hall of Fame finally voted him in.

Not bad for a Brooklyn kid who tried out for the Dodgers in high school, but was told by the manager that at 5' 6' he'd never be a Major League ballplayer.

The manager advised him, he later said, to "Get a shoeshine kit."

The manager was Casey Stengel.

So the fact Rizzuto did make the Majors, and got that MVP, and became a favorite of Stengel's, really rendered almost everything else trivial.

He liked radio broadcasts better than TV, he once said, "because if you make a mistake, they don't know. You can make anything up on the radio."

But you couldn't make this up.

On Aug. 4, 1985, the Yankees declared Phil Rizzuto Day at Yankee Stadium. Among the surprises was a black cow with a silver halo, a reference to Rizzuto's signature broadcast exclamation, "Holy cow!"

The cow, who probably had not spent a lot of time around home plate at Yankee Stadium, took a step forward and knocked Rizzuto down.

"That thing really hurt," he said later. "That big thing stepped right on my shoe and pushed me backwards, like a karate move."

Mantle, as one of the presenters, said Rizzuto was being given a then-massive 45-inch TV set so he could get a good view of the last three innings of all the games he left early.

Scoot over, Ralph Kiner. You've got company.

## Chapter Forty-Three
**Hawkins' No-win No-hitter**

It started out as one of those games only a baseball fan could love and ended up as the kind of game a baseball fan could hate.

Andy Hawkins didn't feel all that great about it, either, being that he threw a no-hitter and lost, 4-0.

But then, it was only through a couple of unlikely twists that he was pitching at all.

July 1, 1990, was a warm sunny day at Comiskey Park in Chicago, with a 16 mile-per-hour wind blowing from right field to left.

The White Sox were riding high, sitting in first place with a 46-26 record.

The Yankees were in seventh place, 28-45 and going nowhere. Even many years later, one name on the scorecard says it all: Steve Balboni was starting at first base.

Andy Hawkins was a free-agent pitcher gamble who came up snake eyes.

The gamble, a year earlier, hadn't seemed unreasonable.

Hawkins had been a sturdy starter in San Diego for most of the 1980s, going 18-8 in 1985 and winning what as of 2014 still stands as the only Padres victory ever in postseason play.

Before the 1989 season, the foundering Yankees signed him to a three-year deal for $3.6 million, which was a lot of money in those days.

The first year he went 15-15, which was respectable on a bad team, though his ERA was 4.80 and he led the league in earned runs.

The second year, 1990, wasn't a charm. By early May he had one win and an 8.56 ERA.The Yankees, who were bad but not that bad, gave up.

On May 8, the team offered him his outright release.

He accepted, and was packing his coffee mug that night when pitcher Mike Witt was injured.

Suddenly the Yankees needed a live arm, however suspect. Hawkins stayed.

He pitched respectably in his next couple of games, though he went into Comiskey Park on July 1 with only that one win and four losses.

That night he became the pitcher the Yankees thought they had signed. He didn't allow a baserunner until he gave up a pair of two-out walks in the fifth.

Meanwhile, White Sox starter Greg Hibbard was perfect through five innings himself.

So the teams had sent up 29 batters before its first baserunner, which made it the kind of game where non-fans whine that baseball lacks action. Real fans, of course, realize that comment misses the whole point.

In any case, Hawkins pitched a 1-2-3 sixth and gave up one harmless walk in the seventh.

The Yankees, meanwhile, finally rustled up the game's first hit, a one-out single by Barry Geren in the sixth. They added another hit, then got two more in the seventh, but didn't get a runner past second base.

In the bottom of the eighth, Hawkins got the first two batters to pop up and the third batter, Sammy Sosa, to ground to third.

Unfortunately, Yankee third baseman Mike Blowers only knocked the ground ball down. By the time he had a handle on it, his throw to first was late.

At first the official scorer ruled it a hit, then reversed the call¬ which was fine with Blowers, who said it was "an error all the way."

Hawkins later said that reversal distracted him. He walked Ozzie Guillen on seven pitches, then walked Lance Johnson on four.

With the bases loaded, he got Robin Ventura to hit a fly ball to left. Deep but catchable, as they say.

When the aforementioned 16 mile-per-hour wind got hold of the ball, however, and left fielder Jim Leyritz—a third baseman doing emergency duty in the outfield—saw it glance off his glove.

By the time he chased it down, all three runners had scored.

The next batter, Ivan Calderon, flied to right. Jesse Barfield dropped that one, too, this time saying he lost it in sun. Ventura scored.

Dan Pasqua then popped up and shortstop Alvaro Espinoza managed to catch it.

So Hawkins still had his no-hitter. He also had a 4-0 deficit, which held up when the Yankees went quietly in the ninth. Balboni reached on an error and Barfield promptly grounded into a double play to end it.

The 4-0 loss was the widest margin by which any pitcher would lose a no-hitter in the 20th century.

And you'd think that would be enough insults for Andy Hawkins, except it wasn't.

The following year, Commissioner Fay Vincent appointed a group named the Committee for Statistical Accuracy.

On Sept. 4, 1991, the committee recommended that a no-hitter had to cover a minimum of nine innings. Vincent agreed.

Since the White Sox didn't bat in the ninth, that meant Hawkins didn't pitch a real no-hitter after all.

In other words, the aftermath was as messy as the eighth inning.

On the other hand, why should that game and Hawkins' luck be any better than the rest of the reason?

Hawkins finished 5-12 with a 5.37 ERA. The Yankees finished last.

Steve Balboni finished the year with a .192 batting average. He was released at the end of spring training in 1991.

## Chapter Forty-Four
### Knoblauch Gets the Yips

When the Yankees traded a quartet of promising minor leaguers to the Minnesota Twins for all-star second-baseman Chuck Knoblauch before the 1998 season, the team thought it had acquired a latter-day combination of Willie Randolph and Steve Sax—a Gold Glove, top-of-the-order speed merchant who would be Derek Jeter's double-play partner for years to come.

Knoblauch would spend only four seasons in New York, and things wouldn't exactly turn out like they planned.

Like with Randolph, the Yankees returned to World Series glory with Knoblauch at second, playing for four straight championships and winning three of them from 1998 to 2000.

But by the end of Knoblauch's Yankee stint he had become like Sax—a second-baseman who couldn't make the short throw to first.

Players have a name for the sudden, inexplicable inability to make a routine throw, whether it's a catcher tossing it back to the pitcher, a pitcher who can't find the plate anymore or an infielder who can't make the play to first base after a ground ball: "The Yips."

It's a rare psychological disorder, but it can be enough to drive a player into retirement. It happened most famously to Pittsburgh Pirates pitcher Steve Blass, a World Series winner and all-star. Known for having good control, Blass woke up one day and couldn't put it in the strike zone anymore.

He walked an average of nearly one batter per inning in 1973 while posting an ERA of 9.85—or more than a run per inning. He was out of baseball a year later, just shy of his 32nd birthday, the Yips forever also coming to be known as "Steve Blass Disease."

Sax, who was afflicted in 1983 while he was with the Dodgers, had it early enough in his career to overcome it, though the Yips would also now be sometimes known as Steve Sax Syndrome.

Knoblauch's Yips turned out to be a permanent case that pretty much derailed all that he had accomplished with the Yankees. His throwing problems had initially surfaced in 1998, his first year with his new team. But his solid bat and speed from the lead-off spot overshadowed his occasional lapses.

By the next year, the condition had worsened. Knoblauch, who won a Gold Glove in his final year with the Twins, committed 26 errors in 1999, too many of them by throwing the ball away. It was double his previous high of 13 errors in '98.

He would hit bottom in June 2000, during a series against the Chicago White Sox at Yankee Stadium. Knoblauch committed three throwing errors in the span of six innings—prompting him to walk off the field and go home in the middle of the game.

Just a few weeks earlier, Knoblauch had contemplated retirement if he couldn't overcome his mental block. "I don't need this," he said after a game in late May in which he threw yet another ball past first baseman Tino Martinez.

"I'm not out here for the money," Knoblauch added. "I'm out here to have fun."

It only got worse. Manager Joe Torre, who along with the rest of the team had expressed nothing but support for their beleaguered second-sacker, put Knoblauch back in the lineup right away.

Torre should probably have given Knoblauch a little more time to clear his head. Two days after his three-error horror show, the frustrated second baseman launched another errant throw that sailed clean over Martinez's head, hit the top of the Yankees' dugout and ricocheted into the stands several rows up, striking an elderly woman right between the eyes.

By sheer coincidence, the woman happened to be Marie Olbermann, a lifelong Yankee fan and mother of baseball broadcaster Keith Olbermann—who, as host of "Game of the Week" that day, saw the incident unfold on a TV monitor in an L.A. studio.

"Her face is a little puffy and she expects a shiner," Olbermann would later deadpan. "Her eyeglasses were broken, as was her confidence in Knoblauch."

Mrs. Olbermann survived; Knoblauch's tenure as the Yankee second-baseman did not. He would soon hang up his infielder's glove and be moved to left field for good, his throws no longer a threat to paying customers.

# Chapter Forty-Five
**The Blauch-Headed Play**

As painful as it was for Yankees fans to witness Chuck Knoblauch's throwing jitters throughout his years in New York, they were in absolutely agony on a cool October night in 1998 over what the second baseman did to nearly ruin the team's 114-win dream season.

Rather, it's what Knobluach *didn't* do that almost caused the bubble to burst on the Bomber's otherwise magical year.

The Yankees had come roaring into the American League Championship Series to face the Cleveland Indians after sweeping the Texas Rangers in the first round of the playoffs, thanks to their vaunted pitching staff.

In a near-complete shutdown of the power-laden Rangers offense, starters David Wells, Andy Pettitte and David Cone together allowed only one run in three games.

For a while it looked like the Yankees would also handcuff the even more powerful Indians, the defending American League champs who had beaten the Bombers in the '97 ALDS in five games after facing elimination.

173

Wells continued his postseason mastery in the first game of the 1998 ALCS in the Bronx, shutting out the Tribe into the ninth inning until Manny Ramirez crushed a meaningless two-run homer off the tiring lefty. The Yankees held on to win, 7-2.

Game 2 was a classic October nail-biter. Cone, a 20-game winner that year, dueled Indians starter Chuck Nagy and the Cleveland bullpen for eight innings. But with the score tied at 1-1, the game went into extra frames with the Yankees desperate for a win. With a victory, they'd be going to Cleveland up 2-0 in the series with a hot Pettitte and Orlando (El Duque) Hernandez, the ageless "rookie" sensation from Cuba, slated to start the next two games.

So much for momentum.

The Yankees, who would leave ten men on base and squander multiple scoring opportunities, finally gift-wrapped the game for the Indians in the top of the 12th inning.

After a lead-off single by Jim Thome off Yankees reliever Jeff Nelson, Indians manager Mike Hargrove elected to have Enrique Wilson pinch-run for Thome, a lumbering, 250-pound slugger who would somehow steal a grand total of 19 bases in his 22-year career.

It was like replacing a tortoise with a snail. Wilson, a reserve middle-infielder nearly 100 pounds lighter than Thome, was nevertheless no base-path burner himself. Wilson never stole more than five bases in a season, 14 in all over his nine years in the majors.

Yet it turned out to be the right move—thanks in large part to one of the biggest brain-locks in postseason history, courtesy of Knoblauch.

The next batter, Travis Fryman, laid down an attempted sacrifice bunt that rolled up the first-base line. Yankee 1B Tino Martinez charged in, fielded the ball, whirled and fired it to first where Knoblauch, who was covering, waited.

And waited.

The throw hit Fryman in the back as he hustled up the line, though he looked to be outside the running lane. As the ball rolled behind Knoblauch and came to a dead stop about a dozen feet away, Knoblauch didn't move.

With glove hand on hip, he looked at the umpire and casually pointed to first base, waiting for Fryman to be called out for interference and the play to be over.

Except it wasn't. And the image of a befuddled Knoblauch, standing there nonchalantly as Indian runners frantically circled the bases and his teammates frantically screamed at him to get the ball, would turn even more bizarre when Knoblauch finally did something.

The second baseman, who was chewing gum, blew a big, fat, pink bubble.

Wilson had by this time rounded third and was being waved home when Knoblauch realized the ball was still in play and chased after it.

Incredibly, he still had a chance to nail the runner at the plate.

Now it was the Indians' turn to look silly. Wilson, who had made a wide turn around third, suddenly stumbled and started to lose his balance. With his arms flapping and his legs buckling beneath him, he looked like a drowning man desperately treading water as he struggled to stay on his feet for the last 80 or so feet to home plate.

Wilson somehow made it, belly flopping to the ground and rolling awkwardly into home head first, a step before Knoblauch's throw.

Fryman would end up on third on a ball that never left the infield, and the Indians would score twice more in the inning, handing New York a stunning 4-1 loss at the Stadium as they headed back home to Cleveland in with the series tied at one-all and momentum all theirs.

"I screwed up the play and cost us the game," said a contrite Knoblauch afterwards. "The guy scores from first…that should never happen on a play like that."

His Yankees teammates said all the right things, of course, defending Knoblauch, blaming themselves for going 1-for-11 with runners in scoring position and vowing to move past the heartbreaking loss.

But the New York tabloids, or course, weren't as forgiving. Especially not when the headline practically wrote itself. "Blauch Head" blared the *Daily News*' back page, with a close-up of Knoblauch pointing helplessly at the bag as the ball just sat on the dirt a few feet away.

It was no laughing matter for the disheartened Yankees, who promptly lost Game 3 and were suddenly down two games to one.

Yet there would be a happy ending after all. The mysterious El Duque, who was either 33 or 36 when he escaped Cuba in a raft or a luxury boat, made his first postseason start and held the Indians scoreless over seven innings in Game 4, an eventual 4-0 win.

The Yankees wouldn't lose to the Indians again, taking the series in six.

And Knoblauch, who was booed mercilessly by Yankee fans after what happened, would redeem himself in the World Series against the San Diego Padres by hitting a huge three-run homer late in Game 1.

The Yankees would go on to sweep the Padres for the first of three straight championships. More importantly, they salvaged a season in which they won a record 125 games including the postseason.

Luckily for the team, Knoblauch never got another chance to fulfill this vow, uttered immediately after his all-time gaffe:

"If I could've done something different on that play, I would've," Knoblauch said. "But I would do it the same way if I had to do it again."

In other words: Once a blockhead…

# Chapter Forty-Six
## The Bloop that Killed a Dynasty

In the inevitable book *Baseball for Dummies*, the dictionary section defines, among other words, "bloop."

That definition reads as follows:

"Bloop: or blooper. A weakly hit fly ball that just makes it over the infield. Also known as a dying quail or Texas leaguer."

The next edition might want to include a link to Luis Gonzalez.

Luis Gonzalez, who played left field for the Arizona Diamondbacks, had a monster season in 2001. He played 162 games, came to the plate 728 times, batted .325, hit 36 doubles, smashed 57 homers, drove in 100 runs, wound up with 419 total bases and scored a slugging percentage of .688.

No one was surprised when he won the National League's Most Valuable Player award. He was a guy who every day all season battered the baseball. He hit it long, he hit it hard.

Then on Nov. 4, on the last pitch of the game, Luis Gonzalez got perhaps the cheapest, most pitiful hit in contemporary baseball history.

It won the World Series.

As it fell in the outfield, several steps beyond the glove of shortstop Derek Jeter, Jay Bell ran home from third base and gave the Diamondbacks a walk-off 3-2 win in Game 7.

To call the ball that Gonzalez hit off Mariano Rivera a Texas leaguer insults everyone who ever played in a Texas league. It was a classic Rivera nightmare pitch, a cutter that ran in on Gonzalez and cracked his bat, forcing a tiny opposite-field popup that Jeter ordinarily would have caught 1,000 times out of 1,000.

But Jeter wasn't playing ordinarily. He was playing on the infield grass, and the real story of that miserable little bloop is the story of why Jeter had to be there in the first place.

After six games of the 2001 Series, an unusually emotional match in the raw wake of September 11, the Yankees and Diamondbacks were tied at three games apiece.

Game 7 pitted the Yankees' Roger Clemens against the Diamondbacks's Curt Schilling, a former Red Sox ace against a future Red Sox ace, both near the peak of their careers.

Through seven innings, it was 1-1. Clemens had left with one out in the bottom of the seventh when Tony Womack singled.

Schilling was still in, and he faced Alfonso Soriano leading off the Yankees' eighth.

The count went to 0-2. Soriano fouled off the third and fourth pitches and hit the fifth pitch out of the park.

It was now 2-1 Yankees, and with Rivera ready in

the bullpen, that looked to be enough.

Rivera at that point had recorded 23 consecutive postseason saves. He had never blown a postseason save.

In the bigger Yankee picture, fans were starting to sniff the sweet aroma of justice.

Back in the 1960 Series, the Yankees outscored the Pittsburgh Pirates 55-27 and lost. In this series, the Diamondbacks were outscoring the Yankees 35-14, yet the Yankees were on the brink of victory.

As Clemens put it to his teammates in the dugout, "We're going to win this fucking thing scoring 14 runs in seven games!"

Rivera took the D'Backs out on 14 pitches in the eighth. Randy Johnson held the Yankees in the ninth.

Mark Grace led off the ninth for Arizona with a single up the middle. But Damian Lewis followed with a bad bunt, too hard and right back to Rivera.

Rivera fielded it, wheeled and threw to Jeter at second. Except the ball tailed away, high to Jeter's left. Jeter might have been able to flag it down, but he tried to keep his foot on the bag and the ball sailed past his glove.

With runners at first and second, the Diamondbacks went to the bunt again. This time it was Jay Bell who bunted too hard and right back to Rivera.

Rivera scooped it up and threw a strike to Scott Brosius at third, erasing lead runner David Dellucci with many feet to spare.

Brosius cradled the ball and took a couple of steps back toward the mound, ensuring the runners wouldn't advance.

Yankees fans and announcer Tim McCarver

wondered why Brosius didn't throw to first and try for a double play, since Bell was not much more than halfway up the line when Brosius took Rivera's peg.

But Brosius played it safe, which brought up Tony Womack, who doubled down the right-field line to score pinch-runner Midre Cummings.

That tied the score and left Diamondbacks on second and third. Since a slow grounder or a routine fly could let Bell come home with the winning run, manager Joe Torre ordered the infield and outfield in.

McCarver noted that was a high-stakes gamble with Rivera, since his cutter jammed batters and often led to shallow bloopers.

It wasn't an issue with the next batter, Craig Counsell. Rivera jammed him with a Cutter and it glanced off his wrist, loading the bases.

Sloppy. But all it did was bring up Gonzalez, who got just enough of an 0-1 pitch to send the ball a few feet past the infield dirt.

It was a good pitch. It was a bad hit. Sometimes that's how the quail dies.

# Chapter Forty-Seven
## The Steal

Somewhere between 15 and 18 million televiewers were watching Game 4 of the 2004 American League Championship Series.

An additional 34,826 were watching inside Fenway Park. Add 25 players on each team, plus groundskeepers, ballboys, umpires, vendors and a few Baseball Annies, and it was a good crowd.

And every single one of them knew that in the bottom of the ninth, Dave Roberts was going to try to steal second base.

What they didn't know, what Roberts didn't know, was that once he succeeded, it would become arguably the most famous stolen base in baseball history.

Yes, even more famous than Jackie Robinson's steal of home in Game 1 of the 1955 World Series, the one where Yankees catcher Yogi Berra insisted for the next six decades that Robinson was out.

Roberts wasn't as famous as Yogi or Jackie. He was just on the right base at the right time in baseball's most intense rivalry.

He was, for three or four minutes on one October

night, the Roadrunner to Yankee pitcher Mariano Rivera's Wile E. Coyote.

Before and after that night, Roberts was a journeyman, a perfectly respectable fourth outfielder whose primary asset in 2004, at the age of 32, was his speed.

That's why the Red Sox acquired him from the Los Angeles Dodgers at the July 31 trade deadline that summer.

The Sox, a team never noted for speed, figured that at some point it might need a stolen base. So Roberts was worth a couple of minor leaguers, and over the last two months of the season he also chipped in as a reserve, coming to bat 101 times in 45 games.

He hadn't played in ten days when Game 4 of the ALCS rolled around and suddenly the Red Sox needed that stolen base.

More to the point, the Red Sox needed a miracle. They had lost the first three games of the series, the third by the score of 19-8. On their home field. That game was stopped after nine innings by the mercy rule.

In Game 4, the Yankees led 4-3 going into the ninth. Three more outs and Boston could crawl back under the blanket of gloom that had been smothering the city since its last World Series championship in 1918.

Nor did the Sox have much reason for optimism, being that Rivera just might have been the best relief pitcher ever.

But Rivera had also pitched the eighth, shooting for a rare two-inning save, and he started the ninth wild, walking leadoff hitter Kevin Millar.

There's a reason they say the one thing a relief pitcher should never do is walk a leadoff batter.

Millar stayed at first just long enough to watch Roberts trot out and replace him.

Robert later said that when he left the dugout, Red Sox manager Terry Francona gave him a wink that told him to steal.

Nice story, but a little short on cred. Roberts might as well have been wearing a lime green psychedelic shirt flashing with the words, "I am going to try to steal second base."

Roberts took his lead. Rivera threw to first, like a boxer coming out and touching gloves.

Rivera threw over again. Robert dove back in. It was a little closer, reflecting the fact Roberts had taken a slightly longer lead.

Rivera threw over a third time. Roberts dove back again, very slightly ahead of a swipe tag.

Roberts, who gets asked about The Steal every day and probably never gets asked a single other question about his baseball career, later said that Rivera's throws loosened him up, shook off his rust, made him feel like he was now fully into the game.

Roberts also said he spent the sixth and seventh innings in the clubhouse, watching video of Yankee pitchers' pickoff moves.

He said that by the second pickoff throw he wasn't nervous. He also said that he was surprised how close the third throw came to nailing him.

After the third throw, Rivera went to the plate, where Bill Mueller was patiently waiting.

Meanwhile, Roberts took off. He got a good jump and needed every millisecond of it, because Yankee catcher Jorge Posada took the pitch in perfect throwing position and uncorked maybe the best throw of his career.

In Francona's autobiography, he said the Red Sox bench coach told him he'd never seen a better throw to second. It was timed in 1.79 seconds.

Unfortunately for Posada and Rivera, Roberts finished the second stage of his 90-foot dash in 1.78 seconds.

Roberts dove in on the outfield side of the bag, headfirst, and his left hand got to the bag a millisecond ahead of Derek Jeter's tag.

A game of inches.

And thus was launched Boston's happiest memory since the original Tea Party.

Mueller singled up the middle. Because Roberts was on second base instead of first, he scored.

That sent the game into extra innings, which ended in the 12th when David Ortiz hit a home run off Paul Quantrill.

The Red Sox then won Game 5, also in extra innings, with Roberts again scoring the tying run as a pinch-runner. This time there was no stolen base.

The Red Sox won Game 6 and then Game 7, becoming the first team in baseball history to come back from an 0-3 deficit in a post-season series and win. They then swept the Cardinals to win the World Series, an achievement of no interest whatever to Yankees fans.

The Roadrunner, though, lives in Yankee lore. He is to Yankees fans what Bucky Dent, oops, Bucky F. Dent, is to Red Sox fans.

# Chapter Forty-Eight
## Worst. Inning. Ever.

On April 18, 2009, under slightly cloudy skies at Yankee Stadium with an unseasonably pleasant game time temperature of 75 degrees, Yankees starter Chien-Ming Wang set down the Cleveland Indians 1-2-3 in the first inning.

In the bottom of the first, Johnny Damon walked and Mark Teixeira drove a 1-1 pitch deep into the right field seats.

For 45,167 spectators, this was baseball the way it was meant to be.

And then the game continued into the second inning.

Indians cleanup batter Travis Hafner led off with a weak ground ball to third. So weak he beat the throw from third baseman Ramiro Pena.

Jhonny Peralta followed with a line single to left. Then Wang's 3-1 sinker to Shin-Soo Choo forgot to sink. Choo sent it into the stands in deep left-center. The Indians led, 3-2.

And that was just the warm up act.

Ryan Garko fouled out to the catcher, the fourth and final out Wang would record this day.

Ben Francisco hit a rocket down the left-field line for a double. Asdrubal Cabrera, batting ninth, singled up the middle to drive in Francisco.

Grady Sizemore doubled to deep right and Mark DeRosa did the same, driving in Cabrera and Sizemore.

Victor Martinez singled to right-center, driving in DeRosa, and that wrapped up the day's activities for Wang.

The Indians said after the game that they saw his sinker was sometimes staying up, so it was just a matter of waiting for the right one.

Wang said it wasn't that dire a problem, that he threw lots of sinkers that stayed down. It's just that the Indians kept fouling them off.

He may have had a point. He threw 53 pitches and the Indians fouled off 15 of them.

Whatever the nuances, manager Joe Girardi signaled for Anthony Claggett, freshly brought up from Triple-A. Just the day before, an excited Claggett had told reporters, "It doesn't get any better than this."

It could, however, get worse.

Hafner and Peralta welcomed him with back-to-back doubles to deep left-center field, Martinez and Hafner scoring.

Choo walked and Garko lined a hard single to center, loading the bases. Francisco struck out swinging, creating a moment of false relief before Cabrera sent a 3-1 pitch way over the fence in right field, clearing the bases and raising the inning's run count to 13.

That tied the record for most runs scored in the second inning of a Major League game, ever. That record stood for exactly five pitches before Sizemore broke it with another home run to deep right-center.

DeRosa struck out, putting this half inning in the record books at 17 batters, 69 pitches and 14 runs. It lasted 38 minutes.

Claggett bravely returned to the mound to allow one more run in the third. He was relieved with nobody out and two runners on base in the fourth.

By the end of the game, the score was 22-4 and Wang was 0-3 with a 34.50 ERA.

Wang was the sad part of the story, really.

He had been a terrific pitcher for two and a half seasons, winning 19 games in 2006 and in 2007 and starting 2008 with an 8-2 record.

Then on June 15, 2008, he tore a ligament in his right foot while running the bases against the Houston Astros. The curse of interleague play. It wasn't considered that serious at first, but it knocked him out for the rest of the season and when he tried to return at the beginning of 2009, well, the Indians happened.

He struggled through the rest of 2009, sat out 2010 and came back as a marginal starter with Washington in 2011 and 2012, then Toronto in 2013. In no season did he win more than four games.

Anthony Claggett would appear in one more game for the Yankees, going one inning. He was waived on Sept. 24 and picked up by the Pirates, for whom he pitched another inning and gave up another run.

That was his Big League career. Three games, 3 2/3 innings, 27.00 ERA. Now that's a cup of coffee.

But because of his role in the second inning on April 18, his name is in baseball's all-time record book. You could look it up.

## Chapter Forty-Nine
### A Stupid Show of Hands

From the Sultan of Swat to the present-day Prince of PEDs, the Yankees have lorded over baseball when it came to home-run power, leading all Major League teams an impressive 38 times.

But while you won't find this stat in any Baseball encyclopedia, the Bombers are undoubtedly the record holder in the dubious category of Most Stupid Self-inflicted Hand Injuries by a Pitcher.

Players taking their frustrations out on inanimate objects after a bad at-bat or costly error is hardly a rare occurrence—no dugout water cooler ever felt safe when Yankee rightfielder Paul O'Neill was in a slump.

But at least O'Neill usually had the presence of mind to use a bat during one of his toddler-like tantrums. Over the past three decades, a trio of pissed-off Yankee pitchers, who would have been well-advised to take a time-out in a corner of the clubhouse after a rough outing, instead somehow thought it would be a good idea to let off some steam by punching a wall with their bare hands

No, they did not feel better afterwards.

Doyle Alexander, a well-traveled righty who won

194 games in a 19-year career with eight teams, was on his second tour of duty with the Yankees in 1982 when he got tagged for five runs in the third inning of a May 6 game against the Mariners. The 7-3 loss not only made Alexander winless in Seattle, but 0-for-the-season so far (in a historic footnote, it was Gaylord Perry's 300th career win).

Pulled after the inning, Alexander was likely just as upset with his defense as he was with his performance. Though he gave up five hits in the inning, including two triples, only one of the runs was earned because of an error by catcher Rick Cerone.

The pitcher promptly lost it once he got back in the dugout. Alexander punched the wall, breaking the pinky finger on his pitching hand. George Steinbrenner likely felt like taking a swing at the righty himself once he heard Alexander—who had signed a four-year, $2.2 million deal—was headed to the 21-day disabled list.

To his credit, though, Alexander took full responsibility for his stupidity and committed a rare act of contrition for a professional athlete—he volunteered to forgo his salary while he was away from the team.

"It's very simple," Alexander said. "What I did was wrong. I can't hold those guys responsible for what I did. They signed me to help them, and I can't with my hand in a cast."

It was a classy move that cost him about $65,000 of a $400,000 annual salary for his two-month stint on the DL—around $160,000 in today's dollars.

But Alexander managed to kill any goodwill he had generated by refusing to stay in the minors to finish a rehab assignment. Clearly not ready to pitch in the Majors, Alexander got bombed in his first game back and received one of the worst public rebukes a baseball player ever got from his own team—though Yankees general manager Bill Bergesch was clearly mouthing Steinbrenner's words.

"Here is a man earning hundreds of thousands of dollars to pitch and then flat refuses to get himself ready. He then goes out tonight and proves to the world that the coaching staff and manager were right," Bergesch said in a statement.

"What Doyle Alexander did to his teammates in Oakland tonight was disgraceful, but typical of the selfishness of some of the modern-day ballplayers."

Alexander's punishment was a swift demotion to the bullpen. Finally deemed worthy of a return to the starting rotation a few weeks later, he got shelled again, prompting Steinbrenner to personally humiliate his pitcher this time. He demanded Alexander get a medical exam to determine what was wrong with his $2.2 million investment.

"I'm afraid some of my players might get hurt playing defense behind him," the Boss said.

A dozen years later another righty starter would incur the wrath of Steinbrenner under nearly identical circumstances. Kevin Brown, by all accounts one of the surliest players ever to don the pinstripes, was in the first of two seasons he would spend with the Yankees when he, like Alexander, took his frustrations out on a wall.

The Yankees were in the midst of a tough pennant race with the rival Red Sox on Sept. 3, 2004, when Brown stormed into the clubhouse in the sixth inning of what would be a 3-1 loss to the Orioles.

Unhappy over his performance that night and

disheartened by an injury-plagued season, the 39-year-old Brown, in the penultimate season of a solid 19-year career in which he won 211 games, should have known better when let loose on the wall.

"Stupidity," said Brown later that night, stating the obvious after breaking two bones in his hand. "I reacted to frustration I'd swallowed all year. There are no excuses. I let it boil over and I did something stupid. I owe my teammates an apology for letting my emotions take over like that."

Stupid, yes, but at least Brown, was smart enough to punch the wall with his left, non-pitching hand.

"My plan is to splint it and pitch. I just pray that my stupidity didn't hurt the team," Brown said.

In retrospect, the team—and legions of Yankee fans—wish Brown would have been stupid enough to rear back and slug the wall with all his might that day with his right hand.

He would return in time to start in the historic ALCS series against the Red Sox in which the Yankees blew a three-games-to-none lead that led to Boston's first World Series win since 1918.

Brown, who couldn't get out of the second inning in Game 3 of the ALCS—the Yankee offense took him off the hook in a 19-8 win at Fenway—was the hapless starter in Game 7 who loaded the bases in the second inning ahead of Johnny Damon's grand slam that sealed the darkest few days in Yankees history.

Six years later, A.J. Burnett, the tattooed right hander who came to the Yankees in 2009 as a heralded free agent, one-up both Alexander and Brown by hurting both his hands.

Upset after being pulled in the third inning of an

eventual loss to the Tampa Bay Rays in a July 2010 game, an angry Burnett slammed his open hands into plastic lineup holders attached to a clubhouse door and cut his palms near the wrists.

"I guess I was fed up," said Burnett.

Probably not as fed up as his teammates, the front office and the fans, who watched as Burnett underwent the worst of his three disappointing years with New York in 2010, in which he went 10-15 with a 5.26 ERA and got rocked in his only postseason start, a Game 4 loss to the Texas Rangers in the ALCS.

As if hurting himself in such a foolhardy manner wasn't bad enough, Burnett made it worse by lying about how he got his cuts, telling the trainers he slipped and hurt his hands while bracing himself for the fall. He finally owned up to the truth after the game, admitting what really happened to a suspicious Joe Girardi, the Yankee manager.

Burnett, who went 11-11 with a 5.15 ERA the following year with a franchise record 25 wild pitches, was traded in the midst of a five-year, $82.5 million after three seasons of maddening inconsistency.

This is how fed up the Yankees were with Burnett by that point: The team gave him away to the Pittsburgh Pirates in exchange for two low-level minor leaguers who never made the majors—and offered to pay $18 million of the $31 million left on Burnett's contract to take him off their hands.

# Chapter Fifty
## The '80s Dynasty That Never Was

On a cold night in January 1996, just a couple of months after the Seattle Mariners had stolen away the first playoff series the Yankees had played in 14 seasons, a minor character on a hit sitcom gave voice to what a generation of frustrated New York Yankees fans had been wanting to tell George Steinbrenner for years.

"What the hell did you trade Jay Buhner for?!" yelled Jerry Stiller's Frank Costanza character on "Seinfeld" to an actor playing a befuddled Boss George.

"You don't know what the hell you're doin'!"

It may have been comedy, but those immortal lines perfectly summed up the tragically failed philosophy of the Yankees' front office (or rather, Steinbrenner's philosophy) from the late 1970s to the early '90s, when the team foolishly and often hastily traded away a clubhouse full of prospects and unproven young players who would invariably go on to blossom for other organizations.

The Yankees, as was their wont, almost always ended up with aging veterans who fell short of expectations.

The result was clearly seen on the field: New York's longest stretch without a postseason appearance since Babe Ruth led the Bombers to their first pennant in 1921. What made it even worse for fans was the fact that within those 13 years without October baseball in the Bronx—1982 through the strike-shortened season of 1994—the Yankees were the winningest team of the 1980s, yet with nothing to show for it but a couple of second-place near misses and too many wait 'til next years.

Think some of those young studs they gave away—especially enough good pitching to fill an entire staff—wouldn't have made a difference in those years when the power-packed Mattingly-Winfield-Henderson teams were just a solid starter or two away from winning it all?

The short answer: We'll never know. But it sure would've been nice to see what the likes of Fred McGriff, Willie McGee, Scott McGregor, Doug Drabek and Jay Buhner would have accomplished had they stayed to form a home-grown nucleus like the Yankees enjoyed in the late-'90s with icons Bernie Williams, Andy Pettitte, Mariano Rivera, Derek Jeter and Jorge Posada.

No look at the inglorious parts of the New York Yankees' otherwise illustrious history would be complete without an examination of what coulda, shoulda and maybe woulda been during the team's darkest decade. Judge for yourself:

**Fred McGriff 1B**
Drafted by the Yankees in 1981, McGriff never played a single game for New York, which shipped him off to the Toronto Blue Jays in 1982 in a five-player swap that netted relief pitcher Dale Murray, 33. The

*Robert Dominguez & David Hinckley*

Yankees hardly missed McGriff initially, as Don Mattingly quickly became a star at first base.

But keeping McGriff and turning him into their everyday designated hitter may not have been such a bad idea, especially after Donnie Baseball's back blew out in 1990 and he was never a power threat again.

McGriff played 19 years for six teams, winning a World Series with the Atlanta Braves in 1995. Oh yeah, he also slugged 493 career homers—the same amount as a Yankee first baseman named Lou Gehrig.

Dale Murray's line in three years with the Yankees: 3 wins, 6 losses and a 4.73 ERA to go with 1 save.

**Willie McGee, CF**
A Gold Glove-caliber, stolen base specialist who hit for high average in the minors, McGee was somehow deemed not worthy enough to be included on the Yankees' 40-man roster, which allowed the St. Louis Cardinals to steal him away in a deal for the immortal Bob Sykes in 1982.

As the Cardinals centerfielder and leadoff man for the next decade, McGee won two batting titles, was the NL MVP in '85, and played in four World Series before retiring after 18 years with a .295 average and 352 steals.

Sykes, meanwhile, never threw a pitch for the Yankees, or any other team, after the trade.

**Doug Drabek, P**
Drafted by the Chicago White Sox, Drabek came to the Yankees in late 1984 as one of the players to be named later in an earlier deal for shortstop Roy

Smalley. The 23-year-old started 21 games for the Bombers in 1986, finishing with an unimpressive 7-8 record and 4.10 ERA, and was dealt that winter to the Pirates in a six-player swap that brought veteran starter Rick Rhoden to the Yankees.

Drabek won a Cy Young as the ace of the Pirates staff in 1990 with a 22-6, 2.76 record, and helped lead Pittsburgh to three straight NLCS appearances from 1990 to1992. He'd play 13 years and win 155 games.

Rhoden, 34 at the time of the trade, won a total of 28 games in two lackluster seasons in New York and retired a year later.

**Jose Rijo, P, and Jay Howell, P**
This is a tough one to call, only because the deal that sent Rijo, a fireballing starter, and Howell, a solid reliever, plus three other players to the Oakland A's before the 1985 season brought back future Hall of Famer Rickey Henderson—just 26 and arguably the most dynamic player in the game at that time.

Then again, Rickey being Rickey, his five seasons with the Yankees were productive only when he felt like playing, and he was shipped back to the A's in 1989 for three players after wearing out his welcome in the Bronx.

Rijo, meanwhile, blossomed into the ace of the Cincinnati Reds team that won the World Series in 1990, with the 25-year-old winning two games against the mighty A's.

Howell went on to become the closer for both the A's and then the Los Angeles Dodgers, where he picked up a World Series ring in 1988.

## Greg Gagne,, SS

From the time Bucky Dent was traded away in mid-1982 to Derek Jeter's Rookie of the Year breakout season in 1996, the Yankees' shortstop position was a revolving door of mediocrity manned by journeymen and aging veterans.

The shortstop role over much of that 15-year span could have quite capably been filled by Gagne, who was drafted by the Yanks in 1979 and traded to the Twins in 1982, along with set-up man Ron Davis, for shortstop Roy Smalley.

Gagne, solid if unspectacular, won two World Series in his 10 years with the Twins before retiring after a 15-year career. Smalley barely spent two and a half seasons with the Yankees before being dealt to the White Sox in the deal that would bring Doug Drabek to the Bronx.

## Rick Dempsey, C, Scott McGregor, P, and Tippy Martinez, P

The deal that shipped Dempsey, McGregor, Martinez and two more Yankees to the Baltimore Orioles took place in mid-1976, but the trade would have repercussions that lasted well into the late 1980s.

And while it didn't seem so at the time, the massive 10-player swap in which the Yankees received pitchers Ken Holtzman and Doyle Alexander, plus three other Orioles, is arguably the worst trade the team ever made.

New York would win the pennant in 1976, its first since 1964, and go on to win back-to-back championships in 1977 and 1978. So losing the light-hitting Dempsey, Thurman Munson's caddy, and some unproven young pitchers was no big deal.

But then Munson was killed in a plane crash in 1979, and the Yankees would wait nearly 20 years before they found another regular catcher with a big bat in Jorge Posada.

Dempsey, meanwhile, grew into a hardnosed, savvy leader who knew how to handle Baltimore's quality pitching staff—not to mention irascible manager Earl Weaver—and played in three World Series, including with the Dodgers in '88, over a 24-year career.

McGregor won 138 games over his 13-year career, including 20 in 1980, and went 18-7 as the ace of the 1983 team that won the World Series.

Martinez became a solid set-up reliever who graduated to closer, saving 21 games in 1983 and winning nine. He retired as an Oriole after 14 years in the Majors.

The Yankees end of that deal? The veteran Holtzman won a total of 12 games in three tough years as one of manager Billy Martin's favorite whipping boys, and the 25-year-old Alexander went 10-5 with a 3.29 ERA in his one season with the Yankees in 1976.

Of course, the front office would have no interest in keeping a solid young starter who proved he could win in New York, and Alexander signed with the Texas Rangers the next year as a free agent. He wound up winning 194 games with 10 teams (including a second round with the Yankees in the early 1980s) over a 19-year career.

**Jay Buhner, RF**
Originally signed by the Pittsburgh Pirates, Buhner in 1988 was a 23-year-old power-hitting prospect with a rifle arm, yet deemed expendable when the Yanks felt

they'd be better off with the left-handed bat of Seattle Mariners veteran Ken Phelps, 33.

Buhner would only go on to man right field in Seattle for the next 14 years and blast 310 career home runs. Though he didn't come into his own until the early '90s, Buhner, given the chance, would have made a nice alternative to Jesse Barfield, the Yankees' regular right fielder during their four straight losing seasons from 1989 to 1992.

(Barfield, of course, came over from the Toronto Blue Jays in another misguided trade for 23-year-old lefty Al Leiter, who would only go on to have a 19-year career, win 162 games and pitch in three World Series with Toronto, the Florida Marlins and the New York Mets.)

Phelps, by the way, spent two years in New York, where he hit a grand total of 17 homers and batted .240.

Frank Costanza was right. The Yankees didn't know what the hell they were doin' for a very long time.

# Acknowledgments

Robert Dominguez would like to thank Lori Perkins and Paula Conway for the opportunity to see his first book come to life; Maria Caleca and Danielle Dominguez for their assistance and support; the Daily News' Kevin McDonald and Mike Dabin for their generosity; the B&B Boys Club members for sharing his rabid devotion to the Yankees through good times and bad, and his cousin Vivian Garcilazo for taking him to his first Yankee game in 1969.

Besides his wife Fran, who has let him indulge his baseball habit over the years, David Hinckley would like to particularly thank Robert Hancock and Robert Levinson, with whom he has enjoyed many long conversations about the New York Yankees.

# About the Authors

ROBERT DOMINGUEZ became a lifelong Yankees fan while growing up in the South Bronx in the shadow of the old Yankee Stadium, home office for many of his fondest childhood memories: Playing Little League in the park across the street where the new Stadium now stands, sneaking into countless games once the ushers left the gate, and thinking Bobby Murcer was even cooler than Joe Mannix and John Shaft combined.

As a writer/editor for the *New York Daily News* for nearly 25 years, Robert's had a chance to meet many of the former players he grew up idolizing. But he considers the full-count walk he worked against Ron Guidry while writing a story on Yankee Fantasy Camp as perhaps the shining moment of his journalistic career.

DAVID HINCKLEY discovered baseball in the summer of 1956, when he was 7 years old. His team was the Brooklyn Dodgers. On Oct. 8 of that year, he raced home from third grade to ask his mother what had happened in the fifth game of the World Series, which had been tied 2-2. His mother, who was not a sports fan but had dutifully listened to the game on his behalf, looked up from her ironing to say she wasn't sure, but she thought one team didn't get any hits. That was the moment at which David realized that no matter what team you rooted for, your baseball universe would include the Yankees.

A severe shortage of talent prevented him from taking his own baseball dreams anywhere, though one summer he did lead the Northern New Jersey Newspaper League in triples. Fortunately, journalism didn't set the bar quite as high as baseball, so he spent 50 years in that field, most of them with the *New York Daily News*.

# Other Riverdale Avenue Books You Might Enjoy

### *The 50 Greatest Red Sox Games*
By Cecilia Tan and Bill Nowlin

### *The 50 Greatest Dodger Games of All Time*
By J.P. Hornstra

### *Bases Loaded: Baseball Erotica*
*Edited by F. Leonora Solomon*

### *The Hot Streak: A Baseball Romance*
By Cecilia Tan

www.ingramcontent.com/pod-product-compliance
Lightning Source LLC
Chambersburg PA
CBHW070034100426
42740CB00013B/2688